Hours in the Wallace Collection

By Philip Hendy

Assistant to the Keeper and Lecturer, in the Wallace Collection

WITH AN INTRODUCTION BY

S. J. Camp, F.S.A.

Keeper of the Wallace Collection

WITH 16 ILLUSTRATIONS

DUCKWORTH

3 HENRIETTA STREET, LONDON

First Published - 1926

Made and Printed in Great Britain by
The Camelot Press Limited
London and Southampton

CONTENTS

LIST OF ILLUSTRATIONS

PREFACE

THE Wallace Collection was brought together by three generations of a great family, two of whom subordinated all other pleasures in life to its acquisition. Though to this end they spent their fortunes with a prodigality that amazed and disgusted their contemporaries, it remains for succeeding generations a monument to their taste, foresight, and discrimination.

Francis Charles Seymour-Conway, third Marquess of Hertford (1777–1842), was already rich when he married Maria, daughter of the Marchesa Fagnani, a fatherless child who inherited the fortunes both of George Selwyn and of the Duke of Queensberry. The breaking-up of many famous Dutch collections at the beginning of the nineteenth century provided him with an opportunity to gratify a taste for painting of the Dutch School, and to add to the few pictures left at Manchester House by the second marquess many examples of rare quality. Prices then were low, and a superfluity of fortune remained for an indulgence in social splendour and a dissipation that provoked the satire of Thackeray and the caustic wit of Disraeli. The Marquess of Steyne in *Vanity Fair* and Lord Monmouth in *Coningsby* are only literary figures, but it is probable that the sensational life of the marquess furnished the model.

In Richard Seymour-Conway, the fourth marquess (1800–70), æsthetic tastes outran all others. The son of a man whose extravagant entertainments rivalled those of the Prince Regent hated society, and cared nothing for what passed in the outer world. Although possessed of abilities that Peel thought might have carried him to the place of Prime Minister, the fourth marquess withdrew from politics after his succession in 1842, and, living as a recluse in Paris, proceeded to indulge the one great passion of his life. The mild enthusiasm of the father for the Dutch School gave place in the son to a passionate devotion to French art. He acquired *at unheard-of prices* the gems of the great collections that were dispersed between 1841 and his death in 1870. As a result, Hertford House to-day contains not only superb examples of the Italian and Spanish schools and a series of English portraits of the first rank, but the finest collection in England of French eighteenth-century art. *I only like pleasing pictures*, wrote the recluse in Paris to his London agent, and it is no surprise to find that the art which is so largely concerned with the easy pleasures of life should have held first place with him. The present volume deals only with pictures, but the whole art of the eighteenth century in France appealed to the marquess, and the furniture he acquired can be compared in quality only with that in the Louvre.

Richard Wallace (1818–90), a natural son of the fourth marquess, inherited in his turn the passion for collecting. The gaps left in the Dutch collection of the third marquess were filled, and additions made to the French School, but sheer lack of wall space precluded further buying of pictures. Wallace however, possessed a finer sense of craftsmanship than either of his predecessors, and it is to him that we owe the museum element. He purchased *en bloc* the medieval *objets d'art* of the Comte de Nieuwerkerke for 400,000 francs, and for £73,000 the arms and armour of Sir Samuel Meyrick.

But without the generous act of a donor what was to become a *storehouse of the imagination of our race* [1] might have been dispersed, or have remained (for the greater part) in Paris. Although Wallace had endured the siege of 1870–1, and had spent two and a half million francs in alleviating its distresses, he became alarmed at the excesses of the Commune which followed, and decided to remove the collection to London. To contain it Hertford House was reconstructed, and it was then that the project of a museum for the public benefit appears to have taken shape in his mind. But Hertford House, being held on a Portman lease, could not be bequeathed, and it was realised that another building might have to be erected at great cost and endowed. This difficulty deterred Wallace, ill-health followed, and nothing more came of the project. A will of a few lines, made in 1880, left everything to his

[1] *The Uses of an Art Gallery*, D. S. MacColl, Manchester, 1912.

dear wife, Amélie Julie Charlotte. The end came in 1890, and four years later Lady Wallace fulfilled the desires of her husband by bequeathing the collection to the British nation. It was a happy circumstance that left the giving of the greatest collection of French art in England to the hand of a French lady.

Hertford House is without architectural interest, but its history is linked with that of the founders. Built in 1776 by the Duke of Manchester, it passed on his death to the Spanish Ambassador, being centred in the Spanish quarter of that day. Later the Comte St. Aulaire took it for the French Embassy, but his occupation must have been short, for it was in the possession of the second marquess before 1810. Ackermann made a drawing for his *Repository of Arts* in 1813, which shows the central portion much as it is at present. A fashionable town house in the days of the Regent, and of the second and third marquesses, it shared the literary celebrity of the last as *Gaunt House* and *Monmouth House.* Abandoned by the fourth marquess, it remained closed until the reconstruction of 1872–5, when its first title of *Manchester House* was changed by Wallace as a tribute to the Hertford family. Further reconstruction followed upon its acquisition by the nation in 1897, but it did not assume its final shape until 1913–20, when two upper floors were replaced by offices and three additional Galleries. The erection of a *special museum in a central part of London* was a condition of the bequest that recalls the difficulty felt by Wallace, but it will be agreed that no more fitting repository for the life's work of three founders, and the gift of so generous a donor, could have been found than the house wherein they lived. As we cross the threshold may we be inspired with a little of their love for *pleasing things*, and carry with us as we go one thought of gratitude for so noble a gift. To aid us in our appreciation there can be no more stimulating volume than the present, which supplies in a continuous form the substance of many lectures given by Mr. Philip Hendy at Hertford House.

S. J. CAMP

To

MY FATHER

Hours in the Wallace Collection

CHAPTER I

THE FIRST AGE OF MODERN PAINTING

The Italian Renaissance

In the Wallace Collection no great period of art is represented earlier than the seventeenth century, an age when art was in maturity over a great part of Europe; but this modern European art, and the thought which it expresses, has its origin in earlier ages and in a more contracted sphere. Italy was its birthplace and the Renaissance its long and brilliant birthday, and it is worth while attempting to catch even such a brief glimpse of the Italian Renaissance as is afforded by the few pictures in Gallery XVII (on the first floor).

A thousand years before the Italians had thoroughly dispersed the cloud of darkness which had settled over the ruins of the Roman Empire, Greek civilisation had attained a perfection never actually realised by the Italians. Art is the expression of the mind, and the mind can only find such expression when it has knowledge and has learnt how to co-ordinate and control what it knows. The Greek love of order and definition, of the perfect relation of the part to the whole, is completely realised in sculpture and architecture, the most concrete forms of expression. But the Greek mind was able to express itself and to control nature so completely because it set upon its knowledge of nature very definite limitations. We can look back upon Greek civilisation only with envy at the clarity and order of its ideas, and at the balance and symmetry with which they are expressed in bronze and marble, but the Greek, if he could have looked forward to to-day, would be astonished at the extent of our knowledge and at the technique of oil painting, a more elaborate form of artistic expression than he could ever have contemplated. Our own age has reached an unprecedented extent of knowledge in a hundred different spheres which have been scarcely explored before, but until the present our discoveries have only caused us to be more restless, and will result in only a tithe of the happiness and tranquillity they might bring, if the age of experiments and discoveries is not succeeded by one which learns how to organise and control them to the human will. Such a new age may have to discover a form of expression even more complicated than that of oil painting.

But between the oil painting of the last three centuries and the bronze and marble of the ancient world stands the fresco of the Italian Renaissance—a more contracted sphere of expression than that of oil painting, a more widely expressive technique than that of the Greeks. For when, in Italy, the mind began to grow light with knowledge again after the period of the Dark Ages, the outlook was more complicated for the artist. The Florentines especially were banded together in the small and compact city state which makes human intercourse so lively and so productive of ideas, but, together with the rest of Italy, they were also members of the huge Empire of the Christian Church, which demanded a spiritual allegiance transcending their relations with one another and awoke in them vaguer emotions and aspirations difficult to reconcile with the keenest logic and the most clear-cut ideas. The fashionable and the learned worlds strove to revive all the forms of pagan life and art. Scholars studied and popularised the Greek and Latin authors; dilettantes discussed philosophical questions in academies deliberately modelled upon the Greek plan; the forms of Roman architecture and sculpture were revived and mythological stories of classical gods and goddesses and scenes from Roman history were depicted upon Italian walls. But all these things were done a little self-consciously; few Italians succeeded in becoming entirely pagan, and the Church remained the greatest patron of art, demanding the expression of ideas which could not be expressed in classical forms. St. Francis and Savonarola wielded more power than any of the Greek philosophers.

Thus the Italian artist was torn by doubt and

hesitation from the beginning, and even the Florentines could not find complete expression in sculpture, the medium for the concrete and the definite. Donaletto and Michelangelo, the two great sculptors, never attained the perfect and tranquil harmony of great Greek sculpture, but they came nearer to the satisfactory expression of those spiritual and emotional longings whose nascent expression in Greek sculpture coincides significantly with the decline of Greek civilisation. But these two are in a minority among Italian artists in the choice of their medium. Fresco painting brought more of the world into the sphere of representation, and wider and vaguer emotions within the possibility of expression. It was thus the medium chosen by the body of Italian artists.

The Boy Reading, by Foppa, is a very typical example of an Italian fresco composition of the fifteenth century. The boy immersed in his studies probably represents scholarship, and the bench on which he sits is inscribed with the name of Cicero, a good example of the Italian tribute to the classical world. A Milanese artist, Foppa worked at some distance from the vital current of art which flowed in Florence. But he is nevertheless primarily interested in the linear construction of this room and the arrangement of the little boy's contour within its rectangle. Directed from Florence, the Italians recognised that artistic expression was an intellectual problem, however spiritual or emotional the impulses which originally gave it rise, and from the first the great figures in the history of Italian art set themselves to conquer, one by one, the problems of construction and perspective whose solution brings the power to represent solid three-dimensional objects upon a flat surface.

Drawing is the simplest and the first means by which forms can be realised on a flat surface, and fresco painting became, in the hands of the Italians, an elaborate and powerful form of coloured drawing with great vehemence of expression. It is not painting in the modern sense; line, not colour or tone, is the fundamental means of expression; and it was primarily by means of line that the full power of the Renaissance was built up. The fragment of fresco by Luini which hangs next to the Foppa is an excellent instance of fresco painting upon a larger scale, cut as it is from his largest and most important series of pagan decorations. Luini is not a figure of great proportions among the giants of the Italian Renaissance. Like the other Milanese painters of the time, he succumbed to the influence of Leonardo da Vinci's oil paintings, and imitated his Madonnas *ad nauseam* in a sticky elaboration of light and shade. Two examples of his oil paintings hang on the same wall, and their weakness of colour, drawing, and general expression is in strong contrast with the freshness and simplicity of this fresco head. While he hopelessly misunderstood oil painting, in fresco Luini developed considerable strength and richness of handling. In the modelling of this girl's features, and still more in the arrangement of the hair, one may see how directly expressive his drawing becomes.

Luini's *Head of a Girl* is only a fragment. Foppa's *Boy Reading* is an architectural scene of limited dimensions. It is in Bianchi Ferrari's delightful pagan *Idyll* (illustration) that one finds a wider glimpse into nature and so a more instructive example of the limitations of fifteenth-century painting. Bianchi is a minor artist, and the school of Modena to which he belongs is a provincial one, but he reflects accurately enough the main currents of contemporary art. The figures are his predominant interest; they occupy the greater part of the panel, and are thrown so far forward that the legs of each are amputated a little quaintly by the frame. Their contours are clear cut and strongly emphasised, and the painter has given his most careful attention to rendering the full roundness of their forms. It is not for any lack of expression that Bianchi would be called a "primitive"; there is an idyllic charm in the whole scene, and many painters in more mature ages would have been glad to express so much by the modelling of a hand. But his idea of a picture is not complete. The figures are out of relation to the remainder of the scene. The landscape is a background to them; it does not contain them. Nobody would ever expect them to get up and walk away into the distance. In this very distance the delight in modelling completely absorbs the painter. Each little hill is an artificial shape, and they are arranged one behind the other in obtained in fresco, and colours, too, took on a new luxuriance such as they could not have on the dry surface of a wall. The Van Eycks themselves had a more passionate sympathy with the humble forms of nature and with the less gorgeous aspects of humanity than many of the great Italian artists, but they had not the clarity of the Italian intellect or the boldness of the Italian attitude to life. Nor were they succeeded in Flanders by men capable of developing their ideas. But the methods of the Van Eycks soon made their way to Italy and became alternatives to those already accepted. Bianchi combined with his tempera in this picture a limited amount of oil without much understanding of its potentialities. But greater men, like Piero della Francesca and Leonardo da Vinci, had already begun to use the richer shadows and more luminous colours of the oil technique to intensify the solidity of their forms. In their pictures line no longer claims the first attention and contours are modified by the atmosphere. But the majority held to the fresco technique, and Raphael and Michelangelo gave strength to their figures by their contours more than by their light and shade. It remained for the Venetians, who had never assimilated the old method with any success, to find expression for their more emotional point of view in the development of the oil technique.

Cima's *St. Catherine*, which hangs next to Bianchi's picture, shows how oil painting was used by the Venetians in the early sixteenth century. The

BIANCHI FERRARI: AN IDYLL.

[p. 24.

diminishing order of size, to create an appearan
of distance. Other artists by this time had arrive
at a far more scientific arrangement of line
perspective, but linear perspective is only o
aspect of distance as it appears to us and the mo
exactly mathematical perspectives of this time oft
appear less real than those arrived at by mo
accidental means. In fact, only a part of natu
can be represented by line. Line cannot real
for us the whole expanse of space and the mo
distant aspects towards which man was steadfas
pushing his interest and curiosity. Even with t
human form the illustrative power of line is limit
Only youth is graceful in outline, yet old age be
on its shoulders deeper emotion, and has perfecti
of another and less tangible kind. A hundred thi
in nature have beautiful significance and u
shape, and many of the artists of the Renaissa
who had the deepest and most spiritual emoti
to express turned away from the fresco
its lines in search for new means of express
For in the meantime another technique, dire
opposite to fresco in character, was gaining gro
in power and popularity. This was the use of
paints, which had been brought to a high p
of expression by the Van Eycks in Flanders e
in the fifteenth century. Its predominant c
acteristic was a great luminosity, by which
realities of light and shade could be rendered. G
expression could be gained in it by the subtle fu
of delicate gradations of tone such, as were not t

BIANCHI FERRARI: AN IDYLL.

[p. 24.

diminishing order of size, to create an appearance of distance. Other artists by this time had arrived at a far more scientific arrangement of linear perspective, but linear perspective is only one aspect of distance as it appears to us and the most exactly mathematical perspectives of this time often appear less real than those arrived at by more accidental means. In fact, only a part of nature can be represented by line. Line cannot realise for us the whole expanse of space and the more distant aspects towards which man was steadfastly pushing his interest and curiosity. Even with the human form the illustrative power of line is limited. Only youth is graceful in outline, yet old age bears on its shoulders deeper emotion, and has perfection of another and less tangible kind. A hundred things in nature have beautiful significance and ugly shape, and many of the artists of the Renaissance who had the deepest and most spiritual emotions to express turned away from the fresco and its lines in search for new means of expression. For in the meantime another technique, directly opposite to fresco in character, was gaining ground in power and popularity. This was the use of oil paints, which had been brought to a high pitch of expression by the Van Eycks in Flanders early in the fifteenth century. Its predominant characteristic was a great luminosity, by which the realities of light and shade could be rendered. Great expression could be gained in it by the subtle fusing of delicate gradations of tone such, as were not to be obtained in fresco, and colours, too, took on a new luxuriance such as they could not have on the dry surface of a wall. The Van Eycks themselves had a more passionate sympathy with the humble forms of nature and with the less gorgeous aspects of humanity than many of the great Italian artists, but they had not the clarity of the Italian intellect or the boldness of the Italian attitude to life. Nor were they succeeded in Flanders by men capable of developing their ideas. But the methods of the Van Eycks soon made their way to Italy and became alternatives to those already accepted. Bianchi combined with his tempera in this picture a limited amount of oil without much understanding of its potentialities. But greater men, like Piero della Francesca and Leonardo da Vinci, had already begun to use the richer shadows and more luminous colours of the oil technique to intensify the solidity of their forms. In their pictures line no longer claims the first attention and contours are modified by the atmosphere. But the majority held to the fresco technique, and Raphael and Michelangelo gave strength to their figures by their contours more than by their light and shade. It remained for the Venetians, who had never assimilated the old method with any success, to find expression for their more emotional point of view in the development of the oil technique.

Cima's *St. Catherine*, which hangs next to Bianchi's picture, shows how oil painting was used by the Venetians in the early sixteenth century. The drawing of this figure cannot be compared even with that of Bianchi's figures ; beside the latter's moving treatment of his youth's upraised hand St. Catherine's fingers are utterly without shape. The advance is in the region of luminosity ; the folds of the saint's dress absorb or reflect the light with great variety and richness of tone, and the painting of her jewels is another instance of the study of rich textures which delights the Venetian painter. But the conception of the whole picture is even more conventional than that of any of the others we have noticed. St. Catherine is even more frankly regarded as a sculptured figure. Though made of flesh and blood and clad in richly luminous draperies, she is set upon a pedestal of carved stone within an architectural embrasure. The landscape is far below her, and bears no relation whatever to her existence. Light and shade, colour and texture, which are best rendered in oil paint, are primarily romantic in their effect and cannot find their full intensity within conventional designs.

TITIAN

It was Titian, in the next generation, who finally broke up the old formalities of composition, and with the richness of his light and shade and of his colour obtained control of elements hardly discovered to any previous age. In combining the colour and luminosity of the oil technique with the large scale and free handling of fresco he invented about ninety-five per cent. of the modern technique of oil painting, and set the modern mind free to express every aspect of its sympathy and knowledge.

The *Cupid Complains to Venus*, attributed to him, in Gallery XVI (which runs the whole breadth of the building at the back of the first floor), shows an entirely novel conception of painting. Conventions still linger, such as the arrangement of the mountains in lessening order of size, but the figures take their place in the landscape in a new fashion. They seem to be immersed in the richness of the atmosphere. Colour is Titian's first interest in developing his new attitude towards nature. The mere luxuriance of colour in the red robe of Venus and in the blue of the distant hills and lake is a new means of expression, and the relation of the colours to one another forms another method of composition which binds together the whole scene. The eye is led to the full intensity of the blue mountains by softer suggestions of the same colour in the quiver flung upon the foreground, in the cool shadows of Cupid's wing, and in the gradually deepening tone of the lake ; these enveloping gradations of blue are in perfect sympathy with the rich mass of crimson in the dress of the central figure, and the two gorgeous colours are stimulated by contrast with the mellow browns and olive greens of the trees and landscape. A more detailed instance of the new expression is the Cupid's wing. For the first time we find no interest in the actual shape; only the barest indication of contour can have been made before the painter fell to applying its full richness of texture and tone. There is intense beauty in the mere application of the paint, in its diversity and the relevance of each stroke. One touch suggests the solid pinion, another the transparency of the feather, and each has a variety of tone which gives the whole passage an extraordinary richness of effect. Scholars were long prevented from attributing this picture to Titian because of the feeble drawing of the figure of Venus, but as the painters of this period have been studied with laborious care during the last quarter of a century no personality other than Titian's has emerged capable of bringing colour and texture to such a pitch of expression. The very difficulty experienced with those problems which were solved first by the older schools of painting seems only to emphasise the absolute novelty of Titian's point of view. His endowment with means of expression quite unsuited to the old formulæ forced him to remodel the entire conception of painting for himself and it is consequently only in his comparative maturity that his pictures begun to show his full capacity. It was fortunate for the world that Titian had a long span of life allotted to him. He lived for ninety-nine years and during the century—all but a few months—of his life continued to expand his ideas and perfect their expression. The *Pieta*, now in the Accademia in Venice, which he was painting when death overtook him, is perhaps the most expressive of all his works.

In his earlier years he strove to express a gentle, idyllic spirit of paganism, and his pictures glow with a pattern of brilliant colours. As he grew to old age more disturbing emotions came to possess him; a more passionate romanticism is expressed less through colour than by contrast of light and shade. The full powers of Titian's old age, or comparative old age—for he was in his eighties when it was completed—is seen in the great *Perseus and Andromeda* (illustration) on the opposite wall of the gallery. The amazing beauty he created merely by the rendering of the textures is seen in the figure of Andromeda, where the rich and transparent skin seems to glow with the warmth of life itself. As a piece of flesh-painting it is almost unrivalled, even among Titian's own works. The canvas itself, under the paint, is used to enrich the sense of texture throughout the whole picture, while every stroke of the brush brings life to its details. The shackles which bind Andromeda's foot and the shells upon the foreshore are admirable examples of the power of Titian's brush to give reality with a few deft touches, while the very ease and rapidity with which they are called forth convey an extraordinary sense of vitality. The technique of oil painting is already perfected. The old joy in a pattern of positive colours has given way in order to express a more dramatic point of view; a subtle gradation of tones over a more complex and subdued hue gives a tremendous power in the rendering of light and shade. The intensity of the atmosphere seems to swallow up the whole scene. Andromeda is shrouded with vibrating shadows which hide the contours of her figure and intensify the modelling of its surface, while the seascape at her back is ominous as no other seascape before Turner. No arrangement of forms is necessary to create it : a cavernous effect of distance is rendered by sheer handling of the atmosphere. Dramatic expression has reached an unprecedented pitch.

Yet Titian is still bound in some respects by the traditions of the Renaissance, and anyone who is searching for a more personal degree of expression or a more complete logic of design might find in this picture much that is inconsistent. The naked human figure still occupies too predominant a place for complete realism and is shown rather for its own splendour as a decoration. Andromeda, in fact, breaks into the logic of the whole scene. In a landscape of tremendous depth she is thrust forward so as to occupy the full length of the canvas at the side. One cannot examine figure and landscape without consciously altering the focus of the eye, and so one cannot take in the whole scene at once and experience the full drama of the incident. The characters themselves are not fully subordinated to the dramatic idea and the heroine poses lightly for effect, regarded by her painter primarily as a decorative *motif* ; she floats in the air in spite of her rock-embedded shackles, and has only a coquettish glance for Perseus in the thick of his encounter with the dragon, which may or may not deliver her from a horrid fate. The lighting of the scene is equally illogical, though the balance of deep shadow against a brilliant glow enormously enriches the decorative effect. With the sun setting faintly behind a darkening horizon at her back, Andromeda's lovely body is brilliantly illumined from the front. Perseus not only receives little encouragement from his heroine in his superhuman task, but he is given an impossible feat to perform in the arrangement of the composition. Andromeda is immediately to the front of the picture, the dragon writhes its dreadful body in the middle distance at least fifty yards from the shore, yet his antagonist, whose arm is raised over his head to deliver a blow, has his ankle inside the cave on a level with Andromeda's arm. The motion of his body balances perfectly the swaying curves of the large figure, but the perspective would have been ridiculed by a Florentine. The picture is ransomed from confusion by the coherent power of colour and handling and the perfection of the decorative design, but Titian, while he had invented the means of expression, left a host of problems for solution before those means of expression could be given full effect. But the new technique was a weapon of gigantic force, and by the next century was handled all over Europe. In Holland, in Belgium, in France, and in Spain it was wielded by men who concentrated upon particular aspects of life and set themselves

RUBENS: THE RAINBOW LANDSCAPE.

[p. 32.

to solve the new problems created by the genius of Titian.

Rubens

One has only to turn round from the *Perseus and Andromeda* and look at Rubens' great *Rainbow Landscape* (illustration) upon the opposite wall to find a complete realisation of space such as Titian had never attempted. The whole of nature is in this picture ; the figures are reduced to their proper scale, and every detail so subordinated to the whole that development seems already complete and the point of view appears absolutely modern. Yet Rubens belongs also by the date of his birth and by the decorative tradition to the Renaissance. It is he, indeed, who forms the binding link between the earlier age and the maturity of the seventeenth century. He is usually regarded as one among the artists of the mature tradition contemporary with Rembrandt and Velazquez, but his historical significance is that he belongs rather to the generation before, and was, indeed, born the very year after Titian died. It is he who first among non-Italians assimilated the discoveries of the Venetian and disseminated them through his own work or by his enthusiasm in every corner of Europe. The majority of Italian painters had worked within the bounds of their own country or even spent their whole lives in their native town. But here again the change of technique has enormous significance, for, while the nature of the fresco determined that the picture should remain where the painter had executed it, canvases might be despatched across the world. Thus Titian, though he spent almost his entire life in Italy, was able to send a large part of his work, including the *Perseus and Andromeda*, to the King of Spain. A pretty chapter in history was made when Rubens brought back with him from Italy the Italian transformation of a technique which had come to Italy from Flanders. Rubens regarded distance almost as little as we do to-day, and, besides bringing back the new discoveries with him to Flanders and Holland, we find him copying Titian and exhorting the young Velazquez in Spain and travelling to execute commissions in France and England. The mere quantity of his output, though it has not improved his reputation with posterity, must have added greatly to the influence which he exerted. The majority of his large decorations for churches and palaces are the result of a system of organised mass production. He had an army of pupils and assistants, who carried out in a large scale upon canvas the designs which he painted upon little panels, and whose work he finished and corrected before it was finally delivered. Here again he brings an Italian tradition to completion, for the large scale of much fresco decoration had caused a number of famous Italian artists to employ assistants in the actual execution of their designs. The typical modern picture is too personal in expression and too careful in design to allow of such methods. Rubens brought the business organisation of the rapidly developing northern countries to the aid of an Italian tradition.

While the ceilings executed for Charles I in the Banqueting Hall deserve more praise than they usually receive as productions of what we might call Rubens and Company, we are fortunate to possess in the National Gallery an unusual number of splendid examples by Rubens alone. In the Wallace Collection there is a valuable supplement to them in the series of his designs on a small scale. The panel called *The Adoration of the Magi* is Rubens' sketch for the large picture now in the Antwerp Museum, and shows the painter's personality in its purity. He is unpopular with many people for the Flemish exuberance which often borders upon grossness in the larger productions, and even in this small picture the general idea is scarcely religious, with the staring paganism of the giant Magus in the centre—actually one of Rubens' friends got up in fancy dress—in the portrait of the materially proportioned Mme. Rubens who serves as the Madonna, and in the caricatured animals which close the scene. Yet nothing could be more delicate than the pinks and yellows and greys of the central figures rhythmically related to the paler tones of the subsidiary characters. The oil paint is handled with the freedom of a Venetian, but its sparing use upon the creamy ground of the panel is wholly personal to Rubens. Equally characteristic is the certainty with which he completes the composition and handles his space. The kneeling Magus in the foreground leads the eye into the picture with his extended arm, while the four central figures form a circular chain which binds the scene together and defines the distance. This realisation of the space in three dimensions is more complete than anything accomplished by Titian.

The Triumphal Entry of Henri IV into Paris is a small sketch for one of a series in honour of the French King, designed to supplement that in honour of his widow which had been actually completed and now fills the Salon Rubens in the Louvre. This sketch is one of the few of the new series which were carried out, and the almost completed picture now in the Uffizi Gallery in Florence is one of the loveliest of all Rubens' decorations. Again in this little panel the same delicate colours combine with the same lively brushwork and the procession is bound together by an equal rhythm of line. The manner in which Rubens has treated a scene from French history is an instance of the fact that the painter, while exercising a modern technique, owes his main inspiration to the tradition of the Renaissance. Henri IV is crowned with laurels and drawn in a car in the manner of a Roman victor. In Mantegna's frescoes in the Orangery at Hampton Court we are able to enjoy the most complete example of this conscious recreation of a classical tradition. Mantegna, more than any other Italian painter of the fifteenth century, worshipped the spirit of antiquity as he chose to interpret it, and in this series of frescoes executed for the Duke of Mantua he expressed his idea of the grandeur of a Roman triumph. Rubens had been brought up in Flanders among a circle whose culture had as its main feature this passion for antiquity, and equally as an artist and as a man of culture it was his first ambition to find his way to Rome. The first moment in the history of seventeenth-century art is Rubens' arrival in Italy in 1600. But, whether he visited Rome first or not, he soon found that his outlook was best expressed in the art of the Venetians, and it was on the mainland near Venice that he spent the majority of his eight years away from home and found his first important patron. The Duke of Mantua who took the young artist with him on his visits to various Italian cities, sent him upon his first mission to Spain and employed him to decorate, among other places, his palace at Mantua, was a descendant of the duke who had employed Mantegna. The latter artist's *Triumph of Cæsar* was constantly before Rubens' eyes, and his copy in free-hand of one of the series of frescoes is preserved in the basement of the National Gallery. This little design in the Wallace Collection is painted directly under its influence, and shows how Rubens sought inspiration for his decorations in the allegory and fable with which the Italians had commemorated the Roman world.

A more fanciful and more typical use of allegory

is found in the little panel above which represents the birth of Henry IV. The city of Pau, personified in a beautiful but distinctly Germanic lady, presents the child to Mars, who is handing him the sword. Two Cupids bear a shield, while a third little genius in the corner is Sagittarius, for the month of December. In the companion sketch the children of Hymen hover over Henri IV and Marie de Medici to bless their marriage, a marriage which Rubens had actually seen celebrated in a very different manner when he had accompanied the Duke of Mantua to Florence.

His eight years in Italy made Rubens a famous man, and on his return he was instantly made painter to the Spanish Court in Flanders. The next year he married his first wife, Isabelle Brant, whose portrait is downstairs in Gallery X. Though it is vigorous enough, only the head and the hands can be by Rubens; but it has the sentimental interest of having been handed down until the last century in the family of one of his daughters.

Rubens built a house in Antwerp, and set up there his manufactory for producing decorations upon an enormous scale. The painter's organising ability enabled him not only to produce pictures in this manner for every Court of Europe, but to travel and perform much service for his patrons as a diplomatic agent.

The last five years of his life, however, were spent in retirement on his country estate, the Château de Steen. Here he was able to devote himself more fully to landscape painting, and in the face of nature added to his poetry a sincerity of emotion which makes a more certain appeal to modern minds. *The Rainbow Landscape* has all the exuberance of his other works, with its concord of all the emblems of fertility in nature in the luxuriant light which follows the breaking of a storm. The Herculean energy of the painter is shown in the mere vastness of the scene ; a sense of space which has never been equalled by any other man is created by the deliberate arrangement of the great diagonal lines of cornfield and forest, which drive into the heart of the scene, and is finally bound together by the masses of light and shade and the relieving rhythm of the colour. The golden brown of the foreground passes into the blue-green of the distance already promised by the dress of one of the women, and the two colours are relieved by the red of the other woman's bodice, which passes like a riband through the poppies in the cornfield and a dozen minor touches, to be caught up in the brilliant sky. Although he owed much to Peter Breughel, Rubens is the first of landscape painters in the modern sense, the first to realise that nature might stand alone by herself instead of as a background to men. And yet he seems to have brought the art at once to completion. Other smaller landscapes in the Louvre and at Berlin show that he knew as much about the colours of the atmosphere as he did about the construction of a scene. How far he was in advance of his time is illustrated by a remark of Reynolds in one of his discourses to the students of the academy, which might well have referred to the picture in the Wallace Collection: "Rubens often enlivens his otherwise uninteresting landscapes with a rainbow or some other artificial effect of light." Artifice was all that the eighteenth century asked for and almost all that it received; anything to do with nature was classified as "low." What inclines us most to-day to *The Rainbow Landscape* is the completeness of Rubens' sympathy with nature. These men and women coming home from work are the men and women nature loves, stained with her colours, getting their living from her soil. Virgil's ancient sympathy with the tilled fields and their teeming life had been revived to some extent by the Italians of the Renaissance, but it finds complete expression for the first time in Rubens' work. This landscape surveys the whole of pastoral nature, yet it has the balance and symmetry of perfect art.

Rembrandt

But it is only in his landscapes that Rubens realises the drama of reality. He was not only brought up in close contact with the old tradition, but he was too much of a courtier to penetrate deep into human life. It is Rembrandt who broke finally from the decorative treatment of allegory and fable, and found expression for the struggling perplexities of man's existence. By feeding his imagination, not upon the capricious divinities of the classical heavens, but upon the real sufferings and rejoicings of earthly man, he allowed full play to that dramatic sense which in Titian was limited by the conventionality of his subjects. He thus brought to its logical climax the romantic movement which had begun in Venice. To the intense sympathy towards human nature which had appeared more than two centuries before in the Van Eycks, he added the broader vision and more intellectual design which the Italians had taught the world. From the beginning he made it his first object to express in dramatic form the realities of human life. Portraiture thus naturally became with him one of the most vital means of expression, and here again he was further developing a branch of art which had been a mere bi-product in the Florentine tradition, but which had developed in Venice into a deeper and more complex form of art. In the Wallace Collection we are able in a series of pictures, of which portraits are a justly large proportion, to trace the gradual formation of his outlook and the evolution of the technique which he created for its expression.

The two big portraits in Gallery XVI of *Jean Pellicorne with his son* and of *Jean Pellicorne's wife and daughter* were painted not long after Rembrandt had left his birthplace, Leyden, and set up as a portrait painter in Amsterdam, where a plentiful supply of wealthy sitters was to be found. *The Portrait of a Lady* by Miereveldt, who belongs to the generation before Rembrandt and paints in a style not greatly developed from the Dutch and Flemish portraiture of the sixteenth century, hangs conveniently near that of Jean Pellicorne, and makes an interesting comparison. Against the dark and opaque background of Miereveldt's portrait the lady's head is modelled with delicate care, the brushwork, minute and carefully concealed, rendering a complex variety of tones on a surface of enamelled smoothness. The pattern of her ruff is accurately traced against the background, making a decorative *motif* worthy of her rank, but not rendered as it would actually appear to the eye. Her bodice too becomes a mere formality of pattern without form. Such a representation is adequate enough to render a certain sweetness of expression and to form a pleasant decoration, but it could never convey the reality even of inanimate objects, much less the full depths of character and emotion. In the life-size portrait by Rembrandt in which Jean Pellicorne is represented as taking a bag of money from his son, the faces are rendered with the same enamelled smoothness, the ruffs and other finery stand out in the manner expected by a rich sitter, though rendered less laboriously and with more science, and the whole surface of the picture has the traditional enamelled finish. Rembrandt is still using the conventional technique, but the spirit which already underlies it shows a radical change. There is no sweetness about the expression of this portrait; the whole scene is fraught with a restless spirit of vitality. Rembrandt from the very outset of his career launched himself upon a search for the power to render the realities of solid form, and from the beginning strove to achieve it, not by the drawing of contours, but by the building up of a solid structure, as it were out of the atmosphere in which it is enclosed, and by intensifying the contrast of his light and shade. Thus to the brilliant light upon one cheek he sharply opposes the dark half tones of the other, which in turn merge into the deep obscurity of the background. With the cold colouring and the hard surface of the paint the effect is forced and uncomfortable. These black shadows encroach upon the pair from every side, and from them the man leans forward out of the picture with startled intensity. A restlessness seems to pervade the whole canvas ; one feels that the painter himself is struggling violently for an expression he cannot obtain with such means. There is a strong resemblance between this portrait and the famous group known as the *Anatomy Lesson* at the Hague, which was painted about the same time. It was Rembrandt's first commission from a corporation, and forms a landmark in his career. There, even more than in the Hertford House picture, the expression is restless and unhappy to a terrible degree : the figures strain out of the picture with an even more fearful intensity of look and the nightmare is increased by the hardness of their black dresses and the horrid pallor of the corpse.

Everything that we know of Rembrandt apart from his work proves that he was a man of extraordinary passion, but, while his later works show the tranquillity of conscious power, many of his earlier paintings seem to express a spirit in misery because it can find no sufficient outlet. The meticulous use of paint in these pictures stands in the way of free expression, while the colour is still more inadequate both in expression and as a decorative scheme. The warm reds of the face are isolated among the cold greys and blacks, and the white of ruffs and label stands out harshly from the whole, refusing to play any part in the composition. Even the lighting, which is violently expressive in its contrasts, breaks up the composition into separate patches. No wonder that father and son appear ill at ease and seem to hesitate between the business they have in hand and the duty of regarding the painter.

The companion portrait of the wife and daughter is a far happier picture. Susanna is handing her daughter her weekly pocket-money and again the action seems arrested half way and the two gaze out of the picture, but this time with a more tranquil air. The lighting, though powerfully contrasted, seems to envelop the pair instead of separating them and the shadows are warmer and more gentle. The girl's head is indeed one of the most powerful pieces of modelling Rembrandt had yet produced, heroic in its massive simplicity as a portrait by Raphael. There is a tremendous realisation of depth and solidity in the child's heavy dress, with the overskirt drawn back in a rich fold to tie behind. In the skirt which it reveals is a note of colour such as the other picture totally lacks; thin bands of emerald green are contrasted with golden brown. Yet in this picture too, when seen from a distance, the white ruffs stand out with equal over-emphasis to declaim the immaturity of their painter.

But while he was still painting his clients' portraits in this conventional technique, Rembrandt was experimenting ceaselessly in his studio. He painted his own reflection in the mirror in every conceivable mood and with every conceivable manipulation of the brush. The two portraits of himself in Gallery XIV were painted at much the same time as the two big pictures and one another: yet each is entirely different in treatment and in characterisation. The blustering representation of *The Artist in a Plumed Hat* seems to be an essay in rapidity. The brown dress is done with a few smears of treacly paint of which the actual dripping down the surface of the panel manages to convey in one place a suggestion of folds in the costume. The face is coarsely modelled with a rectangular block of light cutting it in half, yet the brusque twists of paint on nose and moustaches give a vivacity which only Rembrandt could impart. The other *Portrait of the Artist in a Cap* is a more careful and elaborate painting. Rembrandt subjects himself to a merciless spirit of experiment and reveals all the brutal side of the character in his peasant face. The colour of cold grey and brown has only the richness imparted to it by the extraordinary power of the light. Against a grey background of intense luminosity the head stands out with great force: yet the atmosphere envelops it with the utmost gentleness, lighting up one side of the face strongly, but touching upon the other here and there with persuasive penetration. The paint is not smoothly treated here, but in the lighted portions is squeezed thickly over the surface and kneaded into a vibrating roughness which interprets the pulsing of the flesh under the eye and holds the light with determination, in contrast with the smoother surfaces of the reflecting background. It is touched with warm red to increase the contrast with the cold luminosity of the surrounding atmosphere.

In these earlier pictures of Rembrandt one feels the power of a burning imagination; but one feels also the search after something which is not yet found, and it would not be easy to say how much positive beauty has so far come of the search.

The little picture in the next Gallery (XIII), painted a year or two earlier, shows, however, that Rembrandt could paint more tranquil scenes even then. *The Good Samaritan* is a tiny panel, but it contains a world of emotion rendered with extraordinary completeness. Christened Harmenz after a famous low church preacher, Rembrandt became the greatest, perhaps the only, interpreter of Protestantism in art. His romantic temperament had caused him to break with the artistic tradition which had found its climax with Raphael and Michelangelo in Rome, and it was in the same spirit that he substituted for the gorgeous decoration with which they had feasted Catholic eyes the scenes of real and humble life in which the Gospel had been enacted. In this little picture the emotions which the original scene would have aroused are re-created with peculiar intensity by the artist's brush. The completeness of the composition, with its arrangement of lines all mounting towards the door, through which the wounded man is to be carried, and the concentration of the light towards the same spot, gives the feeling of isolation from the rest of the world which prepares one for emotion. In the centre the limpness of the wounded man is movingly contrasted with the sturdy cheerfulness of the boy holding the horse and the solid strength of head and shoulder in the man who lifts the sufferer from its back.

We find these emotions expressed in a far more mature fashion in the big *Centurion Cornelius,* in Gallery XVI, whose four life-size figures make it the only picture of the kind exhibited in England. In the interval of more than fifteen years Rembrandt has adopted a rich and glowing colour, which gives a new beauty to his light and shade. His *Night-Watch,* the huge and famous picture finished in 1642, is the second landmark in his life ; it was his next important commission, but it marks an epoch in his career far more because in it he first declared himself a colourist. The great masses of black and yellow and red in which it is planned bring it into continuity with the Venetian tradition. Rembrandt's brother-in-law was a picture dealer and acquired *en bloc* one of the most famous of Venetian collections, while it is even probable that Rembrandt saw on a visit to London, before the *Night Watch* was begun, Titian's great *Ecce Homo*, which the Duke of Buckingham had brought to England.

In the Wallace Collection picture the Centurion himself is clothed in garments which glow with exotic colour. A hundred shades of pink and grey and yellow are threaded in his turban, while his exposed sleeve provides a mass of pink perhaps too brilliant for the quieter shades of the remainder of the picture. The three figures before him, the two servants and a devout soldier whom he despatches to Peter at Joppa, are treated in a more sober fashion with dull scarlet, grey, and mustard yellow, but the broad streaks in which the colour is applied and the greater intensity of the atmosphere which envelops them help to balance the two sides of the picture. These three figures are handled with Rembrandt's full power. The rich touches of pigment convey each one a variation in colour and tone, and each performs its exact office in the masterly construction of the forms. There is a weight and solidity about the heads which the Italians had achieved in fresco, but which had been rarely obtained in oil painting before, and they are set in a depth of atmosphere which conveys profound emotion. With the artist's developed sympathy for colour the light takes on a new warmth and a softness which brings tranquillity at last. It binds all three figures together, yet each is lighted differently to express a separate character. The soldier is an escort not interested in the instructions and, as he stands to one side, the light merely gilds the rim of his dark silhouette. The two servants are of contrasted types; the old man, dogged and unmoved with years of service, waits patiently for his orders, and the light upon his face is softly transfused. But the young man bends forward, cap in hand, zealous to obey, and the light strikes him sharply upon the upper side of his face, darkening the lower half with contrasted shadows and intensifying the eagerness of his attitude. Rembrandt's whole method has undergone a complete change since the painting of the Pellicorne family. The cold thin brushwork has given way to a thick impasto which builds up the substances from the thin transparent glazes of the surrounding shadows. There is an intense use of thick paint which seems to be characteristically Dutch, for no one makes such use of it again until Van Gogh at the end of the nineteenth century.

Rembrandt's life is a tragic one and troubles crowded upon him after a short period of worldly success, the survival of only one of his children, the death of his wife, and his reproval at the hands of his inferiors in character for the conduct of his life with Hendrickje Stoffels, who took her place. He had a lasting fame among other artists and with the discerning few, but his art was vigorously abused by the majority, and he suffered a neglect which he would suffer over again if he were born to-day.

The *Portrait of Titus* (illustration), his only surviving son, was painted probably in the very year of his bankruptcy, but it shows no diminution of his power; his feelings were probably even intensified by the mortification he must have suffered over his outward circumstances. The *Titus* shows in the perfection of his technique the triumphant logic of his ideas. There are no accessories here to divert the attention, nor does any passage stand out. The face is isolated against the dark background of luminous shadow, from which the lighted parts emerge. The mere depth of the painting conveys extraordinary expression, one feels one could put one's hand into the shadows and one's finger into the curls. This intensifies the sense of solidity felt in the lighted part of the head, which is painted in thick, opaque paint applied with such mysterious power that it is only at a distance that it creates the full impression of solidity. The colour is subordinated to the light and shade, yet it is rich and varied within its warm limits of brown and orange and red. The perfect harmony of every element is in striking contrast to the harsh discrepancies of the

REMBRANDT: THE ARTIST'S SON TITUS.

[p. 50.

early portraits at the other end of the room, and in this harmony the ideas of the painter find their full realisation. One could hardly find a more perfect expression of Rembrandt's mentality than this portrait of his son, for in calling forth his utmost emotion it betrays the full subjectivity of his attitude. No boy's face shows such profound expression in actual life, and the extraordinary tenderness which makes itself felt is not so much an emotion actually felt by the boy himself as Rembrandt's own feeling for his son.

Hals

The profound subjectivity of Rembrandt's attitude towards life and the richness of the medium which he evolved for its expression are more easily realised in comparison with the picture upon the same wall by Frans Hals, his famous *Laughing Cavalier*. Hals' interest in humanity is wholly objective. He is entranced by the momentary expression of the passer-by, but never attempts to probe beneath the surface of everyday incident. To catch the instantaneous and to perpetuate it upon canvas was his main ambition, and it is an ambition which demands the keenest perception and extraordinary concentration, if not profound sensibility. *The Laughing Cavalier* is a fine example of Hals' peculiar point of view. The vulgar swagger of this bold gentleman has such freshness that one can hardly believe that the artist did not make use of a camera to "snap" him as he walked into the studio and sat down; such spontaneity demands an extraordinary rapidity and precision of execution, and the effort to render it at least aroused in the painter a sense of the beauty that was to be gained by mere brushwork. But *The Laughing Cavalier* is not a good example of Hals' potentialities from the artistic point of view. The line of the black hat cuts a hard silhouette against the cold grey background and the colouring of the dress lacks any feeling. Every one of the heads by Hals in the National Gallery has not only a more real and less exaggerated expression, but shows a softness of tone and a beauty of handling far in advance of the picture in the Wallace Collection. There is an infectiousness, however, about the expression which makes it an interesting game merely to sit near *The Laughing Cavalier* and count the number of moustachioed men who straighten their backs and twirl their moustaches upon perceiving it. But it is questionable whether their emotion is a particularly worthy one, or whether there is any artistic content in the picture at all. It is not one for which stronger affection is prompted by familiarity.

Velazquez

Rubens, on his first visit to Spain, had written in unflattering terms of his Spanish colleagues, "Dieu me garde de leur ressembler en quoi que ce soit." He cannot have come in contact with "El Greco," who had received his training in Venice and been the first among the Spanish to evolve from the Venetian technique a powerful means of personal expression. But twenty-five years later a second visit in a more distinguished capacity brought Rubens into company with the young Velazquez, not long established at the Court. Velazquez had been influenced by "El Greco" and he had before him the great series of dramatic scenes, including the *Perseus and Andromeda*, painted for Philip II by Titian; but Rubens with his Flemish enthusiasm must have been a valuable stimulus to a more sanguine temperament in appreciation of the possibilities of the colourist technique. Velazquez saw the great painter of world-wide reputation make copies of two of Titian's pictures and heard his prompting to waste no time in visiting Venice. As soon as Rubens had gone, the visit was made.

But Velazquez's temperament was one of slow and thoughtful deliberation. Reserved and silent, he was able to see clearly beneath the romantic enthusiasms of such exuberant figures as Titian and Rubens. He diagnosed acutely the illogicalities of the great romantic artists and he set himself to observe more accurately than any painter had done before, not particular aspects of form or colour or light, but the whole field of vision as it actually appeared to the eye. Compared with Titian and still more when compared with Rubens, he produced little work; but gorgeous decoration was not his primary ambition, and he never developed either the sleight of hand with which Rubens learnt to cover such enormous spaces of canvas or the looseness of touch with which Titian obtained his effects. Though his actual technique was simpler and more direct than that of either painter, he must have deliberated long before he placed each separate stroke. For the perfection of his result lay in the exact notation of every tone and every colour, in contrast to the exaggeration by the majority of artists of particular effects.

Every painter whose work we have so far examined was primarily intent upon the problem of realising to the utmost the solidity of his forms. It is the first problem of every painter who desires to present any appearance of reality, and from the early days of the Italian Renaissance onwards the majority of artists have gained their expression primarily by the emphasis of their power in its solution. Ever since the oil technique had been brought to bear upon the problem, it had been used to exaggerate the contrasts of light and shade by which form is most easily rendered. We have seen this exaggeration come to a climax in Rembrandt, who attained at the same time the highest pitch in romantic expression. In another chapter we shall find Poussin coming to Italy to insist upon a return to linear design, but he attained his perfection of contours and arrangement at an inevitable sacrifice of the emotional and dramatic power of expression rendered by intense solidity and the emphasis of light and shade. Velazquez too, with his reserved temperament and sanguine vision, insisted upon a stricter arrangement of his composition than that of Titian or Rubens. But he demanded also a greater measure of reality and struggled to avoid any of their exaggerations.

Rembrandt had experienced considerable difficulty in adapting his passionate character and intense way of life to the free and energetic society of Holland, and his relations with his fellow citizens did not pass without tragedy. Velazquez lived in the narrowest and most static society of seventeenth-century Europe, and seems to have felt entirely at home. Spanish civilisation represented a determination to perpetuate for ever the *status quo.* Eleven years before Velazquez was born, the Armada suffered its disastrous defeat for no stronger reason than that it was in the command of a man who had no resolution, no command over other men, and had never been to sea before. He was chosen as the leader of the most expensive enterprise in the whole of Spanish history simply because his title was the first in the land, and therefore nobody but he could represent the King. Society was organised in a series of concentric circles and no individual might step out of the circle of his class. In the centre were the King, and the Queen, whose garment could only be touched under penalty of death, even to save her life. While the

Inquisition maintained the inflexibility of religion, not even the noblemen were allowed to send their children to be educated abroad, and a rigorous censorship was established over every book which should come into the country, lest any new idea should penetrate the fastness of the Spanish mind. To the painter the study of the nude was debarred, while his status was lower than in any other country. Velazquez as Court painter received even the intimacy of the King, but only in the privacy of the Palace ; when he attended a public show his place was among the barbers of the Court.

In the royal palace, the very core of this stagnant civilisation, he passed his entire painting life. No one in such surroundings could have been a very passionate Romantic : the astonishing thing is that Velazquez should have found such deep expression through his intense reserve and have maintained such extraordinary freshness of outlook. His manner of painting went through many changes, but from the first it has a firmness and precision shared by no other painter.

Its rigid perfection makes his art unusually difficult to describe, and it is rather by a reminder of the weaknesses of Titian's *Perseus and Andromeda* that one can best appreciate the portrait of *Don Baltazar in the Riding School* (illustration) on the same wall. Titian's passionate illogicalities make Velazquez' scene appear absolutely complete. No detail of colour, light, or drawing is allowed to

VELAZQUEZ: DON BALTAZAR CARLOS IN THE RIDING SCHOOL.

[p. 56.

obtrude itself or to distract. Everything is subordinated to the actual realities of an occular impression. The drawing is not emphasised and the contours are no clearer than they are when we actually take in the impression of an object as a whole ; as the objects represented become more distant, their outlines become less and less distinct. The figures under the wall of the riding-school are indeed merely sketched in with a few light touches and have no outlines at all, but the very manner in which they are sketched is characteristic. A Florentine would have marked their contours first. Velazquez places them as patches of tone, absorbing exactly so much of the light in the atmosphere, for we do not see outlines first, even when we can see them at all. He chooses black for the central figure of the young Prince and for his horse because black absorbs every particle of light and so centres the attention. The horse is a rotund animal suitable for so small a boy, yet there is hardly a gleam of light upon his coat to show the construction of the body, and though his forelegs are raised expectantly in the air, he evidently has no intention of transferring his weight from his hind quarters. The horse's attitude is one of the moment, and the whole scene conveys a single impression of the eye before it has time to examine minor exactitudes and forget the appearance of the whole. Like almost every portrait by Velazquez it represents a member of the Court, actually the little son of Philip IV.

The Lady with a Fan upon the opposite wall is

a rare instance of a portrait of someone outside the immediate circle of the Court, and it has been suggested that this is the painter's daughter who married his pupil Mazo. That it represents a member of his family is made very probable by the existence of two other portraits of the same person. It is a more personal portrait and the reality of general effects has to be sacrificed to a more detailed treatment of the features. But these are built up with the utmost concentration of means: deep shadows are confined to a thin rim round the contour of the face and to the hollow of the eye, and the construction is effected, not by any obvious passage from dark to light, but by the extreme relevance of every touch of paint. Each brings its modification of colour and light exactly suited to the particular angle of the surface which it represents. By these subtle and hardly visible changes in the paint Velazquez differentiates even between the substances beneath the skin. Even in the gloves, while the paint renders exactly the qualities of the leather, it is applied with such skilful modulation that the whole structure of the hand is perceptible beneath. The arrangement shows a sternly perfect design. Nothing obtrudes itself unduly: ribbon and chain and fan each have their duty to perform in making the pattern of the whole. So subtle was Velazquez' process and so reserved the whole character of his art, that they passed almost unnoticed in other countries for two centuries after his death, while the exaggeration of light and shade continued to dominate oil painting. It was only in the middle of the nineteenth century, when the direct line of oil-painting initiated by the Venetians had become exhausted, that French painters drew attention to Velazquez' point of view. The main characteristic which separates the modern age of painting from the tradition of Venice and of the seventeenth and eighteenth centuries is the absence of any forced contrast of light and shade. Of this new tradition, as well as of the simpler technique with which it can be executed, Velazquez is the ancestor and the connecting link with the Renaissance.

Van Dyck

Van Dyck has been left for discussion to the last among the great seventeenth-century painters because it is he who links them with the English painting of the late eighteenth century, though only the last years of his life were spent in England and these were the period of his decline.

His powers had developed with extraordinary precocity, but as the result of an almost feminine sensibility which rapidly wore itself out and abandoned the artist so soon as he lost touch with more vigorous personalities.

Before he was twenty, Van Dyck had set up on his own as a portrait painter, and it was in his earliest years that his portraits exhibited most of the traditional acumen which had put Flemish portraiture in demand all the world over. Yet he painted decorative pictures also, and was soon recruited by Rubens, the generalissimo of the army of Antwerp decorators which included practically the whole talent of Flanders. Those who ordered pictures from the manufactory were soon insisting that he should be among the assistants employed.

It must have been Rubens who familiarised him with the Venetian colourists : the elder painter with characteristic generosity encouraged him to develop the decorative side of his art and gave him the parting gift of a horse when, twenty years later than Rubens, he set out for Italy, to remain there for six years. Genoa, where Rubens also had worked, was his headquarters, but he paid the inevitable visits to Venice and Rome.

Where Rubens was a courtier and a man of the world, Van Dyck was a dandy ; and where Rubens with his more titanic personality copied Titian's work out of his sheer enthusiasm wherever he went, Van Dyck made sketches of Titian's compositions in water-colour and borrowed their *motifs* for his own decorative works. But his enthusiasm was even more unqualified than that of the older painter. Among nineteen paintings by Titian which Van Dyck owned the *Perseus and Andromeda* was one and it cannot be altogether fanciful to find a reminiscence of it in Van Dyck's painting which now hangs on the same wall, *The Portrait of the Artist as Paris.* The action of the head and the expression of the face resemble those of Andromeda, while Van Dyck's concentration of the light upon the figure among the brown shadows and his modelling of the form are closely based upon Titian's practice. The whole quality of his paint is infinitely less subtle, but the rich Byronic effect well expresses the painter's temperament. The *Portrait of an Italian Nobleman* upon the opposite wall belongs also to the period of Van Dyck's residence in Genoa. It is by no means one of his best paintings, but in its arrangement, and especially in the landscape seen over a balustrade, it is an excellent instance of the painter's debt to Titian.

The splendid pair of portraits of Philippe Le Roy (illustration) and his wife were painted after the return to Antwerp, when Van Dyck was at his full power. Philippe Le Roy was Counsellor to the Archduke Ferdinand, the Spanish Governor of the Low Countries, and was an intimate of Van Dyck. That this is among the relatively few portraits signed by Van Dyck may be due to this friendship or to the painter's realisation that it is among his finest works. The simplification of Titian's colour is coupled with a movement and rhythm of line which belong wholly to the school of Rubens and which impart a suggestion of fiery action in harmony with the Grand Manner of seventeenth-century Courts.

The swirling line of the cloak and the silvery ripple of the contours of the greyhound are cunningly used to carry the eye upward in the composition. The life-size full-length portrait creates a difficult problem of arrangement; for, while the natural level of vision is nearer to the feet, the eye has to be drawn upward as unconsciously as possible to the head. Van Dyck solved this problem more successfully than his Venetian predecessors. The lower half of the figure is painted comparatively flat, with very little change of light to suggest the modelling of the legs. The upward movement of the man's attitude does something to attract the eye with it, but it is the dog primarily which acts as a kind of light-conductor and invites the spectator towards the top of the canvas. Upon its rippling lines the silvery light gradually brightens in contrast to the dark dress; on the hand which strokes the head it becomes brighter still, and the eye is led upward by the brilliant white satin under the slashing of the sleeve to the head, where the light is thrown full and strong, making it stand out with all the force of which the painter is capable. The expression of the face is more magnificent than individual, for, as Van Dyck's decorative ability grew, he lost the intense hold on his sitter's personality which had characterised his early work. He had become in the meantime the perfect type of Court painter, much less human and much more splendid. The proud vigour of his forms and the gorgeousness of his decorative schemes satisfied exactly the needs of the great despotic Courts of the seventeenth century and perpetuate their ideal, the Grand Manner.

VAN DYCK: PHILIPPE LE ROY.

[*p.* 62.

With Philippe Le Roy's wife, in the companion portrait painted the following year, Van Dyck did not have an equal success. He seems to have had no great sympathy with this embarrassed child of sixteen who had just been married to a far too gorgeous husband. But it is worth noting Van Dyck's painting of the tiny spaniel which gives relief to the otherwise vacuous lower half of the canvas. Mainly to atone for the dullness of his assistant's work, it is created by the painter out of almost nothing with a minimum number of characteristic touches. The actual shape of each of these strokes, the freedom with which they are applied and the ease with which they create the appearance give a greater pleasure than could be had from a more laborious rendering.

Gainsborough

Yet it is in Gainsborough that the mere handling of the paint reaches its highest intensity and even tends to predominate with its fascination over the other elements of expression. England in the eighteenth century was a far narrower field than that of Titian or Van Dyck ; there was no great tradition behind Gainsborough, and even less demand than there is to-day for the work of contemporary artists other than in the field of portraiture. Though he became one of the greatest and most imaginative of landscape painters, it was only as portrait painter to a society which had no great discrimination that Gainsborough could make a living. Thus, born a Romantic within a relatively small sphere of art, he inevitably devoted himself to obtaining the utmost intensity in the field which was open to him. The handling of the means of expression is an essential part of the effect gained by all painters, but Gainsborough set himself to obtain from it a more obvious appeal than had been made by any of his predecessors.

He did not step immediately into the great current of European art. Though his family had seen better days, his own circumstances were very modest, and he made no great effort to emerge from the obscurity of a Suffolk village. He went to London to study portrait painting under Hayman, and both from him and from Gravelot, the French engraver, he learnt a delicate style of portraiture which he rendered in a more brilliant manner. But, when commissions failed to follow him in his independence, he readily abandoned London, and, having married a lady endowed with a comfortable pittance, settled at Ipswich in apparent content. His portraits continued to show far more brilliance than those of his master, and his landscapes, which were modelled upon the rendering of a very similar countryside by the Dutch artists of the previous century, showed deeper observation and a more determined spirit than their originals. But so long as he remained in Suffolk Gainsborough's was definitely a provincial talent which needed contact with a larger world. It seems to have been only the importunity of a friend which removed him to Bath, where, as a portrait painter who quickly acquired a great reputation, he joined the current of a larger world. It was at Bath that he became acquainted with the work of Van Dyck, and it is through Van Dyck that he attained to a place among the great masters of oil painting. He became the single-minded disciple of the Flemish painter, copying his work continually to within a few years of his death, and dying with his name upon his lips.

The *Portrait of Miss Haverfield* is a charming instance of this devotion. The very colour of the dress—silvery white under a black cloak—is that of the *Philippe Le Roy*, and at the bottom corner a tall foxglove—curiously blue—springs up to give the same relief to the cool scheme with its touch of colour as the red flower in Van Dyck's portrait. This flower in each picture performs almost a social function. In the Van Dyck it gives a note of comparative homeliness to an otherwise cold and formal scene; in the Gainsborough its intimacy helps to adjust the realism of the little figure to the far more sketchy impression of the landscape behind. This very landscape is a fantasy upon Van Dyck, and even the swirl of the cloak is reminiscent of his movement. But the effect is intensified by the lightning actions of the brush which creates it. The landscape is rendered with an electric grace which creates a completely outdoor impression;

this little girl seems to be walking along a path on the edge of a wood, and yet there is nothing there but a few graceful and vivacious touches. It is to effects such as these that Reynolds referred in the essay he read to the Academy after Gainsborough's death; these are "all those odd scratches and marks which . . . even to experienced painters appear rather the effect of accident than design; this chaos . . . by a kind of magic at a certain distance assumes form and all the parts seem to drop into their proper places." How like Vasari's dictum upon Titian's later works, which, "executed in bold strokes and with dashes, can scarcely be distinguished when the observer is near them, but if viewed from the proper distance appear perfect"!

The *Portrait of Mrs. Robinson* (illustration) belongs also to the final period of Gainborough's art, when he had settled in London. Female sitters were often vacuous and uninspiring, but Mrs. Robinson's lively character seems to have called forth the painter's best. The actress, though only twenty-three, was at the height of her fame and fortune. Like many another *demi-mondaine*, she had received a strict religious education, having been handed over to Hannah Moore at Bristol, where she was born. At eighteen she gained instant fame in the rôle of Juliet, and three years later her acting of Perdita brought her the temporary adoration of the future George IV. The portrait was painted before he had abandoned her, and after

GAINSBOROUGH: MRS. ROBINSON.

[*p.* 66.

she had set up a lavish establishment in Berkeley Square. But the very next year saw the tragedy of her life, which is narrated in Mr. Whitley's biography of the painter. Mrs. Robinson can never have had any great affection for her royal admirer, and her heart seems to have been given rather to a Colonel Tarleton, famous for his exploits in the American War, but a little too dashing for a good citizen. On one occasion he had to fly the country because of his debts, and Mrs. Robinson, hearing of it after her performance at the theatre, hastily borrowed the money and set out in a post-chaise to intercept him at the port. She brought him the money, but arrived paralysed from the waist with the cold. She was unable to stand from that year, and her career on the stage came abruptly to an end, when she was at the age of twenty-four. Among the effects of her house in Berkeley Square, which were sold by auction, was this portrait, bought presumably by the agent of the Prince of Wales, for he at a later date presented it to the third Marquess of Hertford.

One has only to glance from this portrait to the Titian upon the opposite wall to realise the continuity of the tradition. The lovely transparency of Mrs. Robinson's skin is clearly produced by the same process which gives such expression to Andromeda's body and such richness of colouring to the whole of both pictures; the romantic manner of lighting by which in each picture the figure stands out from a background of exaggerated shadow is another integral part of the colourist tradition. Gainsborough is still working upon the same lines with the narrower vision of the eighteenth century, but with all the liveliness and grace of style for which it aimed. There was never a more dazzling suggestion of brilliance than is conveyed by the warm ivory of the dress. Gainsborough had copied Rubens also, and the colour-scheme is more reminiscent of his *Rainbow Landscape* than of any of the pictures by Van Dyck. The same warm brown passing into the same blue-green of the distant foliage is centred in the gold and ivory mass of the gleaming dress. The same thread of more positive colour runs through it to bind and relieve the larger masses. The blue ribbon of the skirt is repeated in the corsage and under the chin, and the veins under the dazzling skin of the arms and neck echo the same note in the painting of the flesh. With this pale colour-scheme chosen for the whole composition the painter has been set a problem by the crude vermilion of Mrs. Robinson's lips. But he is fully aware of the danger ; the dog puts out its red tongue in the centre of the picture, and, lower still, Mrs. Robinson holds upon her knee the miniature of George IV in his scarlet coat ; instead of an isolated spot ruining the composition, the red becomes an additional note in the rhythm of the whole.

Romney

Two other portraits of Mrs. Robinson offer an unique opportunity to compare in representations of the same person the three most prominent English portrait painters of the later eighteenth century. Gainsborough brought to bear upon her character the whole romantic power of the colourist tradition. Romney's smaller portrait in Gallery IX is charming enough, but in comparison thinly executed and superficially expressed. The black, pink and grey colour-scheme gives only a certain liveliness of decoration, and the execution, proportionately weak, expresses only a simpering gaiety without suggestion of deeper emotion or of any mental qualities in the sitter. In the Old Board Room which adjoins this Gallery, Reynolds' portrait, though unusually cold, carries a graver distinction. He had prepared carefully for this picture with an oil sketch and several drawings, and with its very simple technique and broad design it achieves admirably the dignity at which he aimed.

Reynolds

Reynolds came of circumstances almost as modest as those of Gainsborough, and his boyhood was hidden even deeper in the countryside. But there the parallel between the two painters comes quickly to an end. Reynolds' father, though a poor

Devon schoolmaster, had been a Fellow of Balliol, and, even before he left Plympton Earl, the son Joshua had come into contact with the larger world. After an apprenticeship to Hudson, a typical London portrait painter with a wholly mechanical style, and a short period of provincial labour at Plymouth Dock, Reynolds found means to visit Italy, and remained there for three years. He came back a cultured man, who had studied at the source and made the acquaintance of the fashionable English world which flowed continuously through Rome on its Grand Tour. When he set up in London he had already received commissions from influential people, and in a few years his position was assured. The characters of Reynolds and Gainsborough were as unlike as their careers. The latter was passionately single-minded in his devotion to the practice of his art. His eager emotions found rapid expression, and demanded his whole attention from the first. Reynolds was interested in theory as much as in practice, and his emotions had to share his life with his intellect. He had a broad circle of literary acquaintances, which included Johnson, Goldsmith, and Burke, and his published *Discourses* show an ability to express himself in writing not usually given to those who find perfect expression in pictorial art. His is the typical English artistic temperament ; for, while he joined an undoubted discrimination to considerable intellectual power, towards his art he was experimental in attitude rather than single-minded in devotion. As an historian he takes a foremost place in European art criticism and a rank far superior to his position as an artist. He was just the man to be President of the Royal Academy at its foundation, for his popularity, his wide knowledge and his determination raised the ambitions of patrons and artists alike, and maintained them during his own lifetime and for a generation after his death. His funeral was like that of royalty or of a great soldier and such as no artist had received in England before, for he had indeed raised painting and the artist, by his devotion and optimism, to an entirely new position.

But his actual production is, in contrast, disappointing. His experiments in technique caused his colours to fade during his lifetime, and Horace Walpole to suggest that he should be paid for his pictures by annuities—so long as they lasted. His knowledge of other schools of painting caused a more fundamental weakness, for his theories led him to believe only in the Grand Manner as represented by Michelangelo and Raphael, and to recommend these as models to the Academicians, oblivious of the fact that the fresco was not a northern technique and that line had never been the most fertile means of expression for Teutonic races. Such a divorce from theory and practice is never healthy, but, though he fortunately made little effort to practise his own doctrines, his manner was inclined to be heavy-handed, and to lose life with the fading of his colour.

The famous *Strawberry Girl*, of which there is a

version in Gallery XVI, is a pathetic instance of the limitations last mentioned: the poor child is only a faded and consumptive image of her former self. Yet he had once said of this picture, "No man could ever produce more than half a dozen original works, and that is one of mine"—a remark rendered still more interesting by the fact that his inspiration for it derived even more clearly from Rembrandt than any of his other pictures, for it is strongly reminiscent of the Dutch painter's *Young Girl Holding out a Medal*, with which he is known to have been acquainted. The *St. John*, upon the opposite wall, is interesting not only as one of his few subject pictures but as an instance of his dual inspiration. Characteristically Rembrandtesque in the warmly tinted shadows which enclose the little figure and in the thick paint in which it is executed, it descends in composition, through Guido's picture in the Dulwich Gallery, from Raphael's *St. John* now in the Uffizi. Each is equally remote from the rugged figure of the Bible. Raphael represents the saint as a young athlete of heroic build; Reynolds as an attractive little boy shouting a gay exhortation. Raphael's figure has the perfect construction of the full Renaissance. The other has the bad drawing but the lively gesture of the eighteenth century. Had every colour except the brown not faded it might still be a delightful picture.

Before Reynolds was commissioned to paint the *Portrait of Miss Bowles*, aged four, the objection was made that his colours faded. Perhaps the artist was warned of this, and avoided his usual practice, for the colours remain and are unusually fresh. The portrait is typical of the painter's work at its best. The background of broadly painted foliage is rich with flashes of orange light, and the little figure is planted down with firm solidity before it. The blue-grey of her eyes and the pink and white of her cheeks are pleasantly reflected in the shot colours of her silk dress, and her expression is warm and lively. Yet this is not more than good, manly portraiture, and the colour and handling appear obvious and coarse beside those in Gainsborough's *Mrs. Robinson,* which hangs next. Reynolds' characterisation of men is sometimes deep and real, but with women and children he does not enter into great sympathy. Miss Bowles has a warm and attractive smile, but only such a smile as is given to kindly bachelors who chuck children under the chin. One may not read her character as one may that of Gainsborough's *Miss Haverfield* upon the opposite wall. As Mr. MacColl once remarked: "Gainsborough is the father, Reynolds only the uncle, of children."

Unfortunately the large number of pictures by Reynolds in the Wallace Collection includes only one portrait of a man and that a not very valuable example. But in Nellie O'Brien the painter found a sitter whom he was willing enough to paint half a dozen times merely for the pleasure of studying her features. The *Portrait of Nellie O'Brien* (illustration) must be the earliest picture by Reynolds at Hertford House, painted before he had taken to the disastrous imitation of Rembrandt's thick paint and not long after he had moved from Great Newport Street into the big house in Leicester Square, which he occupied for the remainder of his life. To see that this portrait was painted a little under the influence of Rubens one has only to look at the hand, with the clasp of its tapering fingers upon the wrist, and the warm red of their shadows ; but Reynolds was never more spontaneous in his manner or more wholly individual in his conception ; the light which glances down upon breast and arm, to balance the warm half-light under the broad-brimmed hat, really seems to have got between the light muslin and the heavy quilting of her gown. It reveals at the same time a solidity which gives great satisfaction and is balanced by the gay touches of blue and pink.

Reynolds in his boyhood had been brought up upon the *Treatise on the Theory of Painting* by Jonathan Richardson, father-in-law of his own first teacher Hudson. Richardson had prophesied in his book that " the ancient, great, and beautiful taste in painting," then evidently suffering a decline in Europe, would be revived in England. There was little justification for his prophecy at the time, and Reynolds' art can hardly be considered more than the tail-end of a great artistic tradition. But in Gainsborough and in Turner, who developed the

REYNOLDS: NELLIE O'BRIEN

[p. 74.

portrait painter's method and gained a predominant place in the evolution of modern landscape, England did at last make one of her rare entries into the art-creating world and produce two painters who rank among the greatest Europeans of their generation and form the closing chapter in the first tremendous age of modern painting.

CHAPTER II

THE FRENCH SCHOOL

We have so far made no mention of that which gives the Wallace Collection its peculiar character—the French decorative art of the eighteenth century. The pictures are from every source, but the furniture with two or three exceptions comes only from France and with its blaze and splendour dominates the entire building. Among the paintings, those of the French eighteenth century, even if they did not outnumber those of any other period or school, would still form the first interest of the collection ; for art of this kind is not to be found in the National Gallery, nor could it ever look other than a cold and pathetic exile on the bare walls of a museum. It is not the outcome of great ideas which stand for all time, but the luxury of a frivolous class : a class which shivers when it leaves the drawing-room. Hertford House contains the débris of the *ancien régime,* salved by a millionaire nobleman who lived unconcerned in Paris while the revolutions which created modern France continued around him. Not long after he had settled there the revolution of 1848 set Napoleon III on the throne and Paris was under siege when he died in 1870.

During these years Lord Hertford devoted himself to reconstructing from the wreckage of her noble families the whole extravagant paraphernalia of old France. The eighteenth century predominates at Hertford House over the other periods of French art, for it is in the eighteenth century that French private luxury reached its full development and became the wonder and the model of the rest of Europe. But there is enough material for a more comprehensive review of French painting and for a glance backward into earlier times.

The Middle Ages

The soul of medieval France had been expressed primarily in architecture and in a form of sculpture designed for architectural enrichment ; consequently French Gothic art can adequately be studied only in the great cathedrals of France. In the Middle Ages the Church was the chief patron of art, and the great Gothic buildings which expressed the medieval faith gave encouragement to glass-painting rather than to mural decoration.

The only great medieval French painter was Jean Fouquet, who showed in his miniature paintings a sense of form and design essentially French and curiously prophetic of later developments in French art. But it is characteristic that the one strong artistic personality of Gothic France should choose a small scale for the expression of his ideas. Great painting demands freedom to express the personality to its full extent, and no such freedom existed in medieval France. While in Italy men might rise from humble origins to any position, however great, and nothing was so much admired as vigorous self-assertion to this end, in France the feudal system strove to maintain fixed strata in society, and to bind men, their children, and their children's children to the class in which they were born

The French Renaissance

But in the fifteenth century the feudal system was in decline; the barriers raised against progress by the nobles were broken down by the murders and confiscations of Louis XI, and the invention of printing did more peaceful work among the rigid dogmas of a hierarchic Church. The keener air of Italy began to blow beyond the Alps, and the free vigour of Italian self-expression captured first the fancy of the Court and then the heart of the nation. The luxury of Italian Courts and the diversity of Italian art offered allurements hitherto unknown to the wealthy Valois kings. Charles VIII and Louis XII imported Italian artists of every description to decorate their Courts in the Italian style; but neither of those kings had personality enough to stand between his protégés and the national tradition of craftsmanship, and to prevent the inevitable disaster of a compromise between opposite ideals. François I (1515–47) determined to be as thorough as any of the Italian despots of the Renaissance, and to exclude rigorously from his new palace every trace of the Gothic tradition. Fontainebleau was the prototype of Versailles; it was to be no jumble of historic buildings enlarged by succeeding generations in a succession of styles, but a complete and harmonious setting for a magnificent Court. Furniture works, tapestry factory and bronze foundry were set up near by to ensure the harmony of their products with architecture and fresco. Every artist, from the designer of the frescoes to the meanest artisan, realised that he was creating only part of a scheme; one finds here the first complete germ of that decorative ambition which welds every branch of French art into a single whole. This is itself a continuation of the Italian ideal. In Holland or England the painter has had little association with the architect or the cabinet-maker. Rembrandt or Turner put the expression of their own individuality before everything, and realised their ends at the expense of decorative tradition. In France each artist has laid less stress on his own individuality, has been more careful to subordinate himself to tradition and to the system of a decorative whole. Throughout the history of French art this aspect has to be borne in mind by anyone who wishes to achieve complete understanding of the French ideal, and no French artist can be studied entirely apart from the general decorative tradition of the period.

In the introduction of the new tradition François relied almost entirely upon foreign painters. Even the execution in fresco of their designs was entrusted mainly to Italian artisans, and no French decorative painter of ability appeared during the sixteenth century. But in the crafts in which the French were traditionally skilled the national genius was naturally more productive. Architecture, sculpture and furniture show how many French artists assimilated successfully the Italian conventions, interpreting them with a wit and grace which were peculiarly French. At the same time Primaticcio and his school took on under French influences a character which makes them certainly as much French as Italian; but they painted few easel pictures, and none of these are to be seen in English public galleries. While in decorative painting Italy had a monopoly, in portraiture she had to share at least a part of her fame with Flanders, and the favourite portrait painters of François came from the north. Of these we are able to glean some knowledge in the Wallace Collection.

"Clouet"

Until recently nearly all the little French portraits of the sixteenth century were grouped together under the name of Clouet, and it is only in the last twenty-five years that the researches of French scholars have isolated the innumerable personalities which had been covered by this name. In Gallery I at Hertford House there is a little portrait of François himself, which seems to be a French adaptation of a well-known portrait by Joos van Cleef, a Fleming whom François is known to have called into France to make portraits of himself and of the Queen. This little adaptation has at least the interest of representing the most vigorous character of the French Renaissance and the most artistic of French kings. This first room in the collection (on the right as one enters from the Front Hall) is arranged primarily to represent the history of the French monarchy, and has portraits in oil of Louis XIV and Louis XV. We know very little more about Joos van Cleef ; he painted few portraits of Frenchmen, and he must have had less success in France than Jean Clouet, who came also probably from Flanders and remained at the French Court to become the father of the portraiture peculiar to the French Renaissance as well as of a more famous son.

Very few oil paintings by Jean Clouet exist, but the only one in England, *L'Homme au Petrarque*, at Hampton Court, is the most delightful of his works. François was far more prolific, but only the life-size *Lady in her Bath* of Sir Herbert Cook's collection is recognised by French scholars as authentic among the many pictures attributed vaguely to "Clouet" in English collections. François Clouet was born on French soil, and is the first painter working in the new tradition who may truly be called French. On his father's death he stepped instantly into his shoes and became Court painter to Henri II (1547–59) and his three sons, who reigned in succession (1559–94) François II, Charles IX, and Henri III. Like his father, he chose as the primary medium of his portraiture the crayon drawing. François Clouet himself was a prolific draughtsman, and similar drawings on a small scale were produced in large quantities by a host of followers and imitators, who often merely copied drawings by François himself. Only the drawings appear to have been done from life, but frequently Clouet himself reproduced them more elaborately in oil. Both Clouets actually painted miniatures upon parchment, and their oil paintings vary in size from a few inches square to life-size. Sometimes the oil reproductions were done by inferior artists; an instance of this is the portrait of Mary Queen of Scots in Gallery IX (on the opposite side of the Hall), where there is a corresponding group of pictures relating to the British Royal house. François Clouet's drawing for this picture is preserved in the Cabinet des Estampes, in Paris, but of the many copies in oil which have survived none are by his hand. Queen Mary played a part, it must be remembered, in the French history of this time. She was betrothed to the Dauphin, and sent to France at the age of six; there she received her whole education, and developed a full sympathy with French life and culture; she seems also to have imbibed something of French Court morality.

Ten years later the marriage took place, and at the celebration of their nuptials Henri II was killed in the lists and Mary's husband, who was of about her own age, became King François II. The two brothers Guise were the real rulers of France, and François died suddenly before he had reigned two years. Very close in manner to François Clouet are two little oil portraits on paper exhibited among the miniatures in Gallery XI (which joins Gallery II to Gallery X). The anonymous author of these little portraits of Jean de Thou and his wife has received the title from French scholars of the "Anonyme Lecurieux," from the Lecurieux album containing the bulk of his drawings, in the French Bibliothèque Nationale.

The best example of French Renaissance portraiture in the collection is the little portrait in oil on panel in Gallery I. It represents Edward Seymour, Protector Somerset, brother of the one successful wife of Henry VIII, and ancestor of the Marquesses of Hertford. The panel bears upon an added strip of wood the inscription, "M. LE COMTE DE HERTFORD." The fact that the inscription is a later addition has caused it to be discounted, but it seems to have been added less than a century after the picture was painted and represents, no doubt, a respectable family tradition. The features resemble closely enough the engraved portraits of the Protector, and can at least be reconciled with the Duke of Northumberland's lovely little portrait, which is also traditionally supposed to represent him. The Hertford House portrait is probably the earliest of all, painted, no doubt, at the time when his sister's marriage to the King brought Edward Seymour the title of Earl of Hertford. Later he became Duke of Somerset. Both titles became temporarily extinct upon the death of the seventh duke in 1750, but the earldom of Hertford was soon revived in the person of Francis Seymour-Conway, who became, a few years later, first Marquess of Hertford, and was great-grandfather of the collector. Protector Somerset, like all distinguished Englishmen of that period, was closely in touch with the Continent and its culture. He employed a French dilettante nobleman named Denisot as tutor to his daughters. These ladies published a collection of panegyric poems, under the title of *Le Tombeau*, upon Margaret of Navarre, sister of Henri II; Denisot painted a portrait for its frontispiece.

This portrait of Protector Somerset belongs to another group of paintings which had also become confused in time with the work of the Clouets, but which have quite independent characteristics of their own. Corneille de Lyon, a Dutchman born at the Hague, was the head of this school, and employed in his studio men who produced inferior copies of his works. All these portraits have the same small dimensions, the same brilliant backgrounds of emerald or azure, and the same lively and delicate handling of the features. No drawings for them exist, and they must have been painted, unlike those of the Clouet school, direct from life. Their general arrangement and handling are more reminiscent of contemporary Flemish and German work, but in their peculiar piquancy they are characteristically French.

There is no more compelling instance of the cogent, all-pervading intensity of the French national character than the rapidity with which these foreign painters—the Fontainebleau decorators from Italy, and the portrait painters from the north—shed the characteristics of the countries from which they came, and developed in their stead a feeling which is absolutely French. One can already speak of the French school of painting. But Renaissance culture was confined to the Court, and between the art of the sixteenth century and that of the seventeenth the break is almost complete; for at the end of the sixteenth century came the disastrous civil wars which divided French Society into armed camps, destroyed the Valois dynasty, and set the Bourbon upon the throne. The Valois kings had represented only the most princely house among an aristocracy which was still largely feudal in its ideals, and so opposed to the modern idea of nationality. The wars which were begun upon religious grounds developed quickly into purely dynastic feuds, and the aristocrats, while they tore France asunder, settled their own fate. Henri IV (1594–1610) was accepted by the nation because he alone could curb the power of outgrown feudalism. The Bourbon dynasty was erected by himself, and, under his son, by Richelieu, over the aristocratic claim for independence, and the French monarchy represented the nation in the seventeenth century as it had never done before.

There is a similar divergence between the art of the two periods. That of the Renaissance was a comparatively exotic culture, confined to the Court; the Italianisation of every art was encouraged and modified by the personal tastes of the King; it did not penetrate deep enough to produce a single artist of outstanding power. There was grace in abundance, but no personality to stand out in Europe. When peace was restored, the widow of the new Bourbon King, Marie de Medici, had once more to look abroad, and Rubens was commissioned to decorate her Palace of the Luxembourg.

Poussin

So far the subjects of the pictures mentioned have been more interesting than their qualities as works of art. In the reign of Louis XIII (1610–43) the first two great French artists appear. French painting had received a check from the political upheavals of the later sixteenth century, but the appreciation of classical and Italian art had increased, and in the reign of Louis XIII had become more understanding. An example of this finer sympathy is the beautiful French bronze relief hung over the inner doorway in Gallery I ; the chain of dancing maidens is based upon the *Danseuses Borgheses*, a famous late Greek or Græco-Roman marble now in the Louvre ; it was removed from the Villa Borghese in Rome for Louis XIII, for whom also this version in bronze was made. The bronze repeats the design of the antique, but in accordance with the French feeling for clean and delicate contours the draperies are perfected, the forms beneath more clearly defined, and the heads entirely remodelled.

At this period the enthusiasm for antiquity attained its climax. Even Holland had joined in the worship of the antique. We look on Dutch art to-day as the antithesis to the classical manner of Italy and France, but Rembrandt was chidden for conceit in imagining that he could do without a visit to Rome, and it was the Italianising painters like Jan Both, Van der Werff and Gerard de Lairesse—painters forgotten to-day—who achieved contemporary popularity and maintained it during the eighteenth century. In Holland it is those who avoided the classical style whom we now admire, but in France it is those who assimilated it best. There no real division of opinion occurred.

Poussin was born when the glorification of ancient Rome had reached its height. He early made an attempt to reach the universal goal, but he could get no farther than Florence and was forced back with empty pockets to Paris. It was there that he shaped his ideals, not so much from classical art itself as from the reconstruction of an imaginary classical world to be found in engravings after Mantegna and Raphael. In England we can study Mantegna's vision of Imperial Rome in the wonderful *Triumph of Cæsar* at Hampton Court. Mantegna and Poussin were equally filled with that vision of a lost ideal past, supposed somehow to have co-existed with the Roman Empire, which has proved so fruitful a source of inspiration to many centuries of European art. The Renaissance viewed as a deliberate revival of the ancient world comes to an end in painting only with the death of Ingres. To Poussin it was a burning reality, and he set out for a second time to Rome with his head filled with visions of an austere and dignified past in which magnanimous heroes stood out from a background of Arcadian simplicity peopled by dancing Satyrs and Bacchantes. Arrived in Rome he found his vision shattered by his Italian contemporaries: Italy was in the full sway of a romantic revolt known to us as the Baroque, a movement which produced many interesting experiments and several artists of immense ability, but which expresses, nevertheless, the decadence of the Italian nation.

A national movement in art reaches sooner or later a definite limit of development and in the perspective of history seems to follow a recognisable course. From the Archaic, when fundamental problems must be tackled with uncompromising directness and severe limitations set to the artist's ambition if it is to achieve a worthy result, it broadens slowly to embrace more and more of life, until it reaches the Classical, when the powers of the nation are consciously at their height. To the Classical succeeds the Romantic age, which tends towards dramatic exaggeration. Soon the colossal weapon, forged by previous generations with pain and restraint becomes a mere means for the display of ingenuity in artificial and complicated designs. For Italian art mortification had set in before the French nation consciously set itself to continue the Renaissance tradition and to rival Italy upon her own ground. The majority of French painters attempted to begin where the Italians had at length arrived: they imitated the mere complexity of Baroque Italy without attempting to realise the fundamental qualities which lay beneath. Poussin is the one French artist who understood the true principle of Classical and Renaissance art. He must have been greatly disgusted by the self-satisfied virtuosity of his Italian contemporaries in Rome and set himself to rediscover purer principles. His *Dance to the Music of Time* (illustration) at Hertford House, in Gallery XVI, has that perfection of contour and colour, coupled with their strict subordination to a simple design, which makes one feel the intellectual power of the artist as one feels it in French painting alone. Poussin appeals to few English people at once. The few great English painters have always striven to express

POUSSIN : A DANCE TO THE MUSIC OF TIME.

[p. 90.

the Romantic and have brought painting as near as is possible to the condition of poetry. This picture of Poussin's holds the very essence of an opposite principle, the insistence upon intellectual clarity of design and upon the subordination of part to whole. The austere subject is such as the Classicists of the seventeenth century worshipped. The four dancers represent four aspects of society, Riches, Pleasure, Poverty, and Fame. Riches will only touch the wrist of Poverty, though gladly clasped by Pleasure; but dance together they all must to the music of Father Time. The swift passing of the hours is echoed everywhere, in Phœbus riding in his chariot across the sky, in the fragile bubbles and the hour glass held by the children and in the terminal figure with its twin faces of youth and age. The subject is treated with a corresponding severity. The figures are designed within a square, whose rigidity is only relieved by the subtle undulation of the line of heads and the rise and fall of arms and feet. They have all the dignity of Raphael's heroic figures in the Vatican frescoes, but they have an added perfection of contour, the result of that exceptional finesse which we have already noticed as a characteristic of French Art. Both the colour and the lighting are coldly subordinated to this perfection of form. The colour echoes the grandeur of Titian, but is less emotional, carefully refined lest we should be tempted to forget the design. The shading is planned with firm simplicity of tone, marking exactly the planes and contours of the figures and of the architectural details, while in the landscape, again, the sense of space is firmly controlled lest the eye should be tempted to wander past the figures. The whole design tends to the condition of a relief and is forcibly reminiscent of the *Danseuses Borgheses*; every detail is exactly defined and perfectly subordinated to the whole design. One is conscious of an intensely intellectual point of view, a clarity of vision which has proved the mainspring of French Art. It appears again quite without explanation in Chardin in the very midst of the luxurious riot of the eighteenth century, and in the French painters of the last fifty years, to whom Poussin has been again the heroic figure which he appeared in the seventeenth century. Between these two great periods of French art, the eighteenth century, as represented by Boucher and Fragonard, stands merely as an interlude, when painting became the pretty handmaid of an aristocracy seeking to raise momentary pleasure into the sole emotion of life.

Claude Lorrain

Claude, the other great French artist of the seventeenth century, interpreted the classical spirit from a more romantic point of view. Like Poussin he made his way to Rome, and the two were near neighbours, influencing each other's work. Beside Poussin he was emphatically a Romantic, though in comparison with modern landscape painters he appears formal and conventional. His *Italian Landscape* hung in Gallery XVI as pendant to the Poussin, is signed CLAUDIUS ROMA, proof not only of Claude's classical affectations, but of the fact that his landscapes were composed for the most part in the studio. They are essentially artificial, created by man for his own pleasure. Claude is often blamed for the remoteness of his attitude towards nature ; but this is to blame the whole of his art, for a melancholy ideal retrospection is the very spirit of his work. His is the spirit that we find in Shelley, a spirit of mourning for an imaginary grandeur that has passed. He has no interest in the real and the present. This is a Virgilian shepherd who pipes in the foreground so careless of his sheep, and a nymph of the woods—no milkmaid —who drives the cows so furiously across the bridge behind. Claude's figures are only the paraphernalia of classicism, and he never achieved success either as draughtsman or colourist. The grandeur of his effects lies in the balance of large masses of light and shade, and in the subtle gradation of his tones. There is a truly classical dignity in the broad contrast of light in this picture and in the suave passage from tone to tone in the blue distance of the lake.

The picture contrasts curiously with Rubens' gigantic *Rainbow Landscape* near by. The latter seems to take in the whole of nature, just as it encloses a space of a vastness which Claude had not the energy or the knowledge to construct. Beside Rubens Claude seems small and mechanical enough, yet he provides a tranquil pleasure for our more sophisticated moods, and so perhaps makes his contribution to the complex of experience which is life.

The Age of Louis XIV

Between the austere scholarship of Poussin or Claude and the frivolous decoration of the eighteenth century artists stands the period of Versailles, when the whole artistic energies of France were concentrated upon constructing the most magnificent stage in the world, upon which the *Grand Monarque* might strut. Versailles was the new Fontainebleau, a background complete in itself for King and Court, carried out harmoniously on a single plan. But King and Court in the days of Louis XIV (1643–1715) were very different from King and Court at the time of François I. In the intervening period France had grown into a modern nation, organised, commercial, conscious of itself. The old aristocracy, who as a ruling class had parcelled out France among themselves and had often produced families, like the Guises, more powerful than the Monarchy itself, had been laid low by the great ministers, Richelieu and Mazarin. Louis XIV represented the nation as no king in Europe before or since. Whatever the vices of seventeenth-century despotism —and they were great enough—it had saved France from something worse, and the nation adored, followed, and ruined itself for Louis XIV. This period of French art can only be studied at Versailles, for art like every other branch of human activity was pressed into the service of the Monarchy. The absence of any examples in England is not greatly to be regretted, for the crushing spirit of the despotism, however valuable in enforcing a national discipline, was disastrous to artistic expression. One may catch a glimpse of the great personalities of the time in the splendid busts by Coysevox in Gallery VIII. The bronze of Louis XIV, though not illuminating as a personal portrait, for this colossal figure hardly suggests a very small man, is a perfect expression of the Grand Manner. The ideal of aggressive domination is excellently conveyed by the flowing Baroque arrangement of draperies and peruque, by the twisted opposition of head and shoulders, and by the restless avoidance of vertical or horizontal lines. A comparison of this with the bust of Charles IX at the other end of the room demonstrates the development of the Renaissance tradition, from simple straightforward symmetry to an elaborate gesticulation. Coysevox learnt his methods from Bernini, the great Italian virtuoso, who spread the Baroque idea over all Europe. Painting underwent exactly the same influences, and Coysevox's terra-cotta bust of Le Brun gives a vivid idea of the little martinet, who organised the decoration of Versailles. As generalissimo of the artistic forces, he drilled and dragooned every painter, and set his mark forcibly upon the whole production of the time. Two pictures by him in the Dulwich Gallery reveal the trend of art during his life. The *Horatius Cocles* of Le Brun's youth shows a careful but unintelligent imitation of Poussin, coldly correct, the buildings conscientiously copied from antiquity. The *Massacre of the Innocents,* finished about fifteen years later, shows all the struggling extravagance of the contemporary Baroque. A young nation setting itself to produce a new art should concentrate upon fundamentals and learn to tackle its problems in its own way. But the close contact of France and Italy caused the French to imitate the complexities of their Italian contemporaries, without understanding the deep science with which the tradition had been built up and which still underlay the finest Italian art. Thus among the huge band of artists no single figure of this time occupies any significant position in the history of painting.

Yet, however disastrous to artistic expression the worship of *gloire* and the homage paid to despotism may have proved, the great activities of this period were not without valuable results. In no other nation and at no other time has the production of art become a serious national ambition as it then became in France. The foundation of the Royal Academy and of the French Academy at Rome under the ægis of the Government was an earnest of this, and gave the artist a new status. He became a member of an important profession, a functionary of the State, where he had been a member of an artisan's guild, or the *valet de chambre* of a king. Moreover at Versailles the artists in various crafts were brought into contact with one another and learnt to work together for the creation of an harmonious ensemble, a discipline which counts for much in the creation of a tradition. But, unfortunately, Louis XIV had not the artistic sense of François I, and for the time being art lost in inspiration what it gained in ambition.

The pictures of such a time can be only of historical interest, and in Gallery I is one of the most interesting of the whole period, Largillière's Portrait of *Louis XIV and his Heirs* (illustration). It is in the first place a dynastic portrait, summing up the history of the Bourbon dynasty during a century. Behind the family group are on the left a bust of Henri IV, founder of the line, and on the right that of Louis XIII, his son, the father of Louis XIV. The latter is seated with the heirs of three generations standing round him. Behind his chair is the Grand Dauphin, to the right his eldest son the Duke of Burgundy, and in the foreground, led by his governess, the King's eldest great-grandson, elder brother of Louis XV, the Duke of Brittany. Besides this dynastic record the picture has the contradictory interest of unusual intimacy. The whole family is in morning dress, the King is seated, and on the table behind is the dish of fruit which, St. Simon tells us, he liked to have near him, to help himself at any time.

Louis XIV is a disheartening instance of the lasting awe which pomp and ceremony can create. But in the last years the estimate of his character has fallen lower with every new historian since Lord Acton pronounced him " by far the ablest man who was born in modern times on the steps of a throne." The great period of his reign was his youth, when the governing force was the great Minister, Colbert. It was before the King took his place at the head of his Counsellors that France saw the enormous development of her economic prosperity, the production of much of the greatest of her literature, and the preferment of art to the foreground of the nation's efforts. Colbert's death and Louis' personal direction of affairs resulted in the curtailment of all these intellectual activities and the sacrifice of growing commercial prosperity to an aggressive and wasteful military policy. As the most brilliant ornament of the State Louis was well enough endowed, his bearing stately and his manners perfectly polished and controlled. But divine infallibility in the direction of a people's destinies belonged to him no more than to our less fortunate Charles I. None of the heirs to the throne represented in this picture had any moral or physical strength and, though it was painted not more than five years before the close of one of the longest reigns in history, every one of them predeceased the King himself. Contemporary rumour attributed their deaths unjustly to the hand of the future regent, the Duke of Orléans. The immediate authors

LARGILLIERE: LOUIS XIV AND HIS HEIRS.

[p. 98.

might well have been the doctors, whose art was murderous enough; but the ultimate cause was undoubtedly the divinity of kings itself. Kings who were almost divine could only marry the descendants of other semi-gods. Like his father, Louis XIV married his first cousin. But nature stepped in to disprove the supernatural, and degeneration quickly followed upon the perpetual intermarriages of Bourbon and Hapsburg.

Nattier and the Eighteenth Century

A comparison of Largillière's portrait with those by Nattier in the same room forms a good introduction to the eighteenth century. Louis and his heirs appear pompous and cold; Nattier's heroines are all softness and intimacy. They exhibit in contrast the social ideals of the later generations. Versailles, with its vistas of vast halls and the suites of solid metal chairs which once adorned them, is the product and the symbol of a purely formal, purely political existence. No distinction is made between private apartments and Government offices —for it was no mere palace of pleasure but the heart of a State, the Whitehall to which one had to go throughout the eighteenth century even to get a passport. There is no private life. Yet the eighteenth century is the period of the evolution of domestic life in the modern sense for every class of society, of the invention of the modern house and modern furniture. These were the result of a conscious reaction from the sombre formality of the seventeenth century and of a new search for intimacy and comfort. Compare the chair upon which Louis XIV is represented as sitting with the actual chair of the middle eighteenth century which stands below the picture. Each is a luxurious type of the fashion of its generation. One has a high back and heavy complicated stretchers a few inches from the ground. It is a chair designed for a definite position, to impose itself in a huge room. The other has a low back and is as light as possible, so that it may be drawn closer to another for easy intercourse. Its covering of Beauvais tapestry designed by Oudry is as gay and light-hearted as can be, and covers a back and seat more comfortably padded than those of any previous generation.

Nattier's portrait of *Mlle. de Clermont* shows the quick reaction which succeeded Louis XIV's death, and echoes the sigh of relief which must have been heard in many a drawing-room. This lady was a princess of the blood, sister of the Prince de Condé who was first Minister to Louis XV (1715–74) after the Regent's death ; but she is portrayed in a manner which Louis XIV would scarcely have tolerated; bare legged, with her ermine gown thrown back to reveal a single shift, which does not reach to her knees, she sits before her bath attended by half-clad negro slaves, *en sultane,* according to a momentary fashion for Turkish affectations which followed upon an embassy from the *Porte*. This portrait, as Mr. Constable once pointed out in a lecture at Hertford House, stands in relation to that of Louis XIV rather as some modern portraits, which seem to represent scarcely reputable ladies, to the dull sobriety of Victorian portraiture. Mlle. de Clermont's love-story was very like a nineteenth-century romance and was indeed recorded in a novel by Mme. de Genlis. Like a Jane Austen heroine, she was distinguished by a fondness for literature and by a character in sober contrast with her flattering circle at Chantilly. She was attracted by the Duke de Melun, the Mr. Darcy of her Court, who stood out reserved and proud among her chattering admirers. But a mere duke was not the man whom her ambitious brother or the King were likely to sanction as a suitor. They were secretly married in a dairyman's cottage at two o'clock in the morning. Only a few days after, while their marriage was still a secret, Louis XV came to stay. During the first morning's hunting held in his honour the duke was killed, and Mlle. de Clermont, having divulged her secret to her brother, vowed to pass the rest of her days in perpetual widowhood.

This early portrait of Nattier's is coldly painted and is without any æsthetic interest. That of the *Comtesse de Tillières* (illustration) painted more than fifteen years later, shows his full charm. His more ambitious pictures, such as the series of pseudo-classic portraits of the daughters of Louis XV reveal all the strident coldness of which the eighteenth century was still capable, but some of the simpler portraits of this type have an inimitable softness of effect. The charming blue of this lady's cape and the soft grey of its fur border and of the background make a lovely setting for an equally gracious expression. Most of us are tired to-day of this chocolate-box species of feminine portraiture, but what gives an interest to Nattier's pictures is that they are the first to attain this particular quality of softness in expression. The portrait painter follows with quick sympathy the new ideals of decoration, and plays admirably his final note of personal intimacy in the concert of modern luxury.

Watteau

It was Watteau who first brought relief from the gloomy conventionality of the Versailles régime. He did as much to create the eighteenth century as any one man could ever do to create an age. We look at him to-day from a false perspective which tends to hide the extraordinary originality of his genius. To us, looking back, he appears merely one among a whole school of artists who recall a past we can hardly believe to have been anything but ideal. But he was the first of these artists, and to his generation he was a realist of uncompromising boldness, the first painter to achieve an acknowledged position in the French

NATTIER: THE COMTESSE DE TILLIERES.

[p. 102.

school, who painted men and women of his own time, dressed in their own silks and satins, enjoying the pleasures of the day. Untouched by the Italian training to which every Academician of the time was subjected, he brought into a deadly conventional school a new breath of fresh reality. It is enough to compare his pictures with those of Le Moyne in Gallery VIII. Le Moyne was the leader of French painting during Watteau's lifetime, and when, sixteen years after Watteau's death, he took his own life after putting the finishing touches to the *Time Discovering Truth,* he was mourned as France's greatest painter. The latter picture is a good instance of the straits to which the Classical allegory had come since Poussin's day. Couched in the grand manner, it had been the subject of every painter throughout the reign of Louis XIV, and down to the Revolution it remained the ambition of every Academician. But it has no real meaning to the painter, and so he can put no life into its representation; drawing, colour, light and shade, are all equally uninspired. For the other picture, *Perseus and Andromeda,* Le Moyne had to draw inspiration from a picture of the same subject by Veronese which is now at Rennes, in Brittany, but was, in the eighteenth century, at Versailles. Le Moyne's modifications merely rob the picture of its original boldness in design, while the colour, equally debased, is handled with unfeeling coarseness. In both these pictures the human figures monopolise the painter's attention. They must be Classical in type—that is, without personal expression; they must be naked or clad only in classical armour or in "abstract" draperies—draperies, that is, which bear no resemblance to dress, and have no value as clothing. Beyond the figure the Grand Mannerists had no interests in nature, and the Academy student toiled before the model day after day without refreshment from any real source of life. Theory there was in plenty, as the Academy was founded not only to organise but to discuss; but discussion was as narrow as practice, and soon degenerated into the formulation of recipes such as that if the right leg was drawn back the left arm must be drawn forward. Elaborate rules were prescribed by Le Brun as to the exact facial muscles which must be tightened or relaxed to give particular expressions. French painting had become utterly dead.

New life could only come from abroad, and one of the interesting aspects of Watteau, who appears to us the most typical of French painters, is that he is really more of a Fleming than a Frenchman, not only in his intense feeling for colour and texture, but actually by birth. Valenciennes, his birthplace, had indeed been taken from Flanders by Louis XIV a few years before he was born and he is technically a Frenchman, but he was born of Flemish parents and brought up where people talked and thought in Flemish and under the influence of the great Flemish painters. Rubens had long been the parrot-cry of the French Academician, and Le Moyne consciously set himself to carry on his tradition. But the Academy had perpetuated only Rubens' vices, and it was Watteau, fresh from the north, who first really interpreted the Flemish tradition in France and brought with it a new vitality into French painting.

In *The Champs Elysées* (illustration) in Gallery XVIII (exactly over Gallery VIII, on the first floor) his greater breadth of view is illustrated in his handling of the landscape. He is not exactly a landscape painter in the modern sense, but he stands alone among French painters of the eighteenth century in the knowledge of how to use nature in her different moods, to interpret the emotions of his human beings. The shadows under these tall trees and the bright patches of sunlight in the glades beyond set the note to this little picture and balance the intense brilliance of the coloured dresses. What vitality there is in the whole scene, how intensely personal are these people after Le Moyne's dead abstractions! It was this very reality which shocked the Academy of the day, and the subjects of Watteau's pictures were considered the one bar to his success. The costumes of his figures are only partly realistic, these ladies wear a simplification of the afternoon dress of the period, but the gentleman who stands to the right is got up in the costume of Mezzetin, one of the figures in the Comédie Italienne. This moderate degree of realism and the intensity with which it was expressed made Watteau undoubtedly the most popular artist of the day, for he expressed the longing that was making itself felt more and more in society for more personal and less conventional forms.

In *The Champs Elysées* there is extraordinary vitality of colour and handling and a scintillating play of vivid light and shade. Watteau is essentially a colourist, and the composition is created by the brilliant contrast of clear colours in the satin dresses of the group of men and women with the warm enveloping shade of the trees. There is a lyrical rapture in the whole scene; all thoughts of yesterday and tomorrow are cast aside for the full enjoyment of the moment's happy mood. French society must have sighed with relief when Watteau expressed so vividly a new ideal which freed it from the chains of pompous conventionality. The *fête galante* became the ideal of a generation and affected French painting for the remainder of the century.

The Music Party, upon the same wall, is a good instance of Watteau's virility. The colouring, the attitudes, the scintillation of light over the delicate silks and satins of the figures, the note of gentle music, have all the preciousness of the eighteenth century; but there is a robustness about these figures that makes them alive and creative of intense emotion. The figure of the guitar-player is perfectly constructed, poised with a sureness which no other French artist of the eighteenth century could achieve. Watteau understood the clothed

WATTEAU: THE CHAMPS ELYSEES.

[p. 106.

figure as none of the painters who toiled before the Academy models were able to do. There are few things harder to draw than a figure clothed in a loose costume which hides the form, yet in *The Champs Elysées* the ladies reclining in their ample skirts are perfectly articulated and pulsating with life ; one feels that they have really sat down and could really get up again, if they wished.

The fantastic side is uppermost in the *Harlequin and Columbine* upon the opposite wall. Watteau received much inspiration from the Comédie Italienne, which, with its conventional plays and stock characters such as Pierrot and Scaramouche, brought to France the lightness of Italian fantasy. His colour can be seen in its most exquisite refinement in Columbine's skirt, where the rich and subtle hue changes constantly under the influence of light and shade It should be compared with *The Fountain* which hangs next to it, where the dulness of touch and the monotony of the colour betrays the fact that it is only a copy of which the original is still to be found.

Comparison of *The Champs Elysées* with the larger variation, the *Fête in a Park*, in Gallery XVI, shows that Watteau is most successful on the smaller scale, but for this and for the fact that he constantly repeats the same figures in different compositions his bad health must be held accountable rather than the limitations of his mind. He suffered terribly from a consumptive malady, the anguish of which tinges his gayest pictures. The intensity of his imagination, the originality of his point of view place him among the great artists; he opened up a new world for his contemporaries, and gave a new lease of life to French art. If Lancret, who followed closely in his footsteps, was never more than a good imitator, Chardin must have owed to Watteau's vital spirit much of his intense interest in the essentials of painting.

The *fête galante* as a theme did not last very long. Descending through Rubens from the Venetians, it had taken in Watteau an intensely personal form and there was no painter possessed of sufficient vitality or imagination to develop it further.

Pater

A study of Pater is mainly valuable as an aid to the appreciation of Watteau; to maintain under such lightness of touch the full individuality of the subject, to give such intense meaning to every feature and every pose—for Watteau poses his figures with a spontaneity unequalled by any other artist—must be one of the hardest problems of painting. When Pater attempts such lightness of drawing or such refinement of colour the result is merely negative. His figures are without individuality, their poses merely conventional, while the colouring and the light and shade express nothing whatever. In

The Bath, in Gallery XIX, we find some solidity and a certain strength, though no variety, of colour, and the *Bathing Party in a Park* in Gallery XXI, another early work, has enough solidity to give it some conviction. But in the set of four pictures in Gallery XX, typical examples of Pater's later style, *motifs* are borrowed from Watteau and subjected to a lifeless rearrangement. Pater, like many a sweated sempstress of to-day, is a pathetic instance of the plodding and painful overwork which produces the gaieties of the fashionable world. One pictures him debonair, gay, and shallow as his pictures, but he died almost as young as Watteau, worn out with the effort to gain a pittance from his art.

Lancret

Lancret was a man of more comfortable circumstances; he imitated Watteau with infinitely greater success and exhibited at the same time a personality richly imaginative beside that of Pater. Unlike the latter, Lancret was not Watteau's pupil, but his contemporary in the studio of Gillot, a coarsely decorative artist who took some part in the evolution of the *fête galante.* Lancret nevertheless learnt more from his fellow-pupil than he did from his master, and he followed Watteau closely in his choice of subjects, continuing the romantic tradition for more than twenty years after his death. Lancret's personality had none of Watteau's intensity, not did he portray contemporary life with so acute an insight. Even more than his colleague, he delighted in the drama and continuously frequented the Comédie Italienne. The individuals in his pictures have far more of the stage in their compositions; their gestures are less spontaneous, their poses more theatrical, but they are often grouped and lighted and coloured with a warmly lyrical feeling, especially in Lancret's youth, when he was more consciously influenced by Watteau. One of the loveliest of the earlier pictures is the *Italian Comedians by a Fountain* in Gallery XX. Lancret's favourite characters are posed in a pyramid as if for their portraits, Pierrot forming the apex with his hands to his splitting sides, Columbine for ever rebuffing Harlequin below. One can almost hear the soft splash of water in the fountain on the right and the whisper of the tall, autumn-tinted trees behind. Lancret is the only painter between Watteau and Gainsborough who could put so much romance into the mere suggestion of a landscape. There is all the vitality of an individual imagination in this scene; the rich warmth of the colouring, with the massing of the light and shade, convey a lyrical rapture worthy of the Venetians of the sixteenth century. Many of his other pictures in Gallery XVIII portray dramatic characters. The portrait of *Mlle. Camargo, Dancing*, actually represents a well-known figure of the contemporary stage. The career of this ballerina is another instance of the transition towards modernity which marks the evolution of eighteenth-century life. The ballet-dancers of Louis XIV's day are portrayed with a headdress two or three feet high, with long skirts, multiplied by many panniers, trailing upon the ground and hiding their heavy, high-heeled slippers. Their costumes can hardly have allowed them to do more than change their positions upon the stage by means of a stately walk. The celebrated Camargo, made immortal by Voltaire, took high kicks of a modern kind, and insisted upon the full freedom of her limbs. With her equally famous rival Mlle. Sallé, she shortened the ballet-dress to a length ending half-way between knee and ankle—still the regulation ballet length—adding newly invented undergarments to make possible her *pas en haut*. She is seen in this little portrait with nothing upon her head but a knot of flowers, but her most important invention of all Lancret does not seem to have dared to show—she is credited by Mr. Cecil Sharpe with the invention of the modern heel-less ballet-slipper. So in this little portrait one finds written the story of the complete modernisation of another art.

La Belle Grecque, upon the opposite wall, may be another personality of the stage ; there are several versions by Lancret's hand, and the lady herself stands as if gracefully acknowledging the applause of her audience. Well placed in the rectangular canvas, her dress is delightful in the subtlety of its red ; the whole picture has a graciousness of which Frenchmen alone have the secret. But the *Pastoral Revels*, upon the opposite wall, Lancret has simply concocted from several of his own earlier works, and the other later pictures in the same room show a sad weakening of conviction and a colouring grown comparatively coarse. The *fête galante* became less and less convincing as the century went on, and artists and patrons alike seem gradually to have lost touch with life. The famous painter of the next generation achieved his fame as a decorator, not as the poet of a mood or the interpreter of life. It is as a purely decorative artist that Boucher represents, far better than Watteau, the real character of the eighteenth century in France.

The Rococo

One often hears to-day sighs of regret for the passing of that glamorous period, with its silks and satins, its gaiety and its gallantry, its atmosphere of a vanished leisure. Yet only at a heavy cost was that leisure obtained. The domestic system of manufacture which then prevailed led to more overwork and to more terrible conditions than even the factory system by which it was superseded. The reverse of the brilliant picture holds the callousness with which a small class reached out after the good things of life for its own exclusive possession, and the sterile conventionality which followed the contraction of the ends of life to merely frivolous enjoyment. Taste there is in such societies, but taste of a very limited kind, which loves elaboration for its own sake and which gauges a work of art by the quantity of labour expended or the richness of the materials used. Ugliness is not a purely modern phenomenon, any more than beauty is a thing of the past; and most of the Sèvres porcelain, a good part of the ormolu-enriched furniture with much of the interior decoration of the eighteenth century in France, can be valued by no other standard than the cost at which it was created.

Never had there been such intense artificiality in the fashionable world. At the time when the dresses were the most costly and elaborate which Europe has ever seen the streets were so filthy that the rich would not set foot in them. Elaborate toilettes of grease and powder and rouge covered features pitted by the ravages of loathsome diseases, and faces which were not often washed. A tiny basin and ewer of pink Sèvres porcelain in Gallery XXI reveal the highest ideals of ablution in the eighteenth century. Baths were so rare that they were commemorated by the painter's subservient brush. Outward show was the only consideration in life, and many of the tables and secrétaires of the period are so minute, so delicately elaborate as to serve no purpose of comfort or convenience. So the eighteenth century appears in contrast with modern times. But a past age can be seen in true perspective only by a comparison with the age that had gone before. If we compare the eighteenth with the seventeenth century, it appears in a far less irrational light. If in the eighteenth century, gentlemen rarely took a bath, Louis XIV, it is said, never took one at all. At Versailles, sanitary conveniences of any kind seem hardly to have been known. In the eighteenth century ordinary domestic life approached far nearer than ever before to our modern ideals, and it was then that the modern house and modern furniture were evolved. It is the great age of furniture and decoration.

Of the furniture of previous ages only a small percentage has survived, because only a small percentage is of any practical use to-day. Much of it was merely formal; little of it was developed enough to satisfy the needs of modern life. This immaturity in utility is proved equally by the immaturity of the design. It has hardly an art of its own, but is an awkward blend of two other arts, architecture and sculpture. The French Renaissance cabinets in Gallery VIII are enough to illustrate these characteristics. The two against the inner wall especially are lovely examples of the French interpretation of Italian ideas during the reign of Henri II, gay and inventive in their design and slender in their proportions. But they are constructed upon entirely architectural principles; pillars at the sides support broken cornices, and one of them is surmounted by an elaborate carved pediment bearing sculptural figures. Their panels are carved with architectural ornament exactly like that upon the façades of the buildings. A glance at any of the furniture of Louis XV style upon the first floor reveals entirely different notions. Furniture has become independent; it has an art of its own. The curving lines of chairs, commodes, and tables, and the *motifs* of their decoration, are new and distinct; they serve admirably the purpose for which they were evolved, providing that ideal mixture of gaiety and comfort which furniture demands. The French rococo design of the early eighteenth century became the model for all Europe. Our own Chippendale style developed from it; in Sweden, Germany and Russia it was more closely imitated. Furniture was ordered from France by every continental Court, and with it travelled the French decorative painter to complete the internal effect. Pictures by Watteau and Lancret decorated the palaces of Frederick II; Oudry worked for the Duke of Mecklenburg-Schwerin, Boucher executed orders for the Court of Sweden. The latter must have regarded himself more in the light of a decorator than with the proper pride of an artist, for he is said to have charged for his pictures upon two scales. The lower secured only an inferior picture, the higher alone persuaded Boucher to do his best. The painters were subordinated to the general scheme of decoration, they were not required to express emotions or to suggest ideas. Even decoration suffered inevitably from the narrowness of general conception, but before its degeneration it had produced something not without value in the evolution of art. Its heyday was the rococo period, when the eighteenth century was still in its youth, still full of the joy of its release from the chains of despotism. It is a period of many vices, extravagant, unbalanced, often coarse, yet it had great vitality and left a permanent mark.

The foundation of the art of the Italian Renaissance had been its interest in construction ; in architecture all the emphasis was upon the structural idea ; in sculpture on the science of anatomy ; in painting the same science was enlarged to include perspective and the construction of a scene. In the seventeenth century came a reaction, and the baroque artists revolted from old ideas of symmetry, seeking the dramatic and the emotional at the expense of the constructional aim. It was against this romantic impulse that we have seen Poussin struggling, and himself returning to an even purer interpretation of the Classical than any Italians had attained. But, though the French Academicians made Poussin their figurehead, they cared little for the fundamentals of his art, and under the influence of the Italians developed a baroque of their own. By the end of the reign of Louis XIV this impulse had taken a purely national form, lighter, gayer, less forceful, but more graceful than its Italian parent. It even achieved a new name—rocaille, or rococo. The old structural style was an intellectual achievement, an idea based on the realities of engineering. The eighteenth century mistrusted ideas and hated realities. It called for a gaiety and movement which would assist it to forget them. The rococo was admirably shaped to this end: it tolerated no straight line, and under its fantastic ornament the structure disappeared. It was at its zenith during the Regency, but the painters of this period, like Watteau and Lancret, were realistic, that is to say that they realised scenes of life, and were not primarily decorative, as were the best painters of the next generation.

Boucher

Of these Boucher is the first. It is the rococo spirit which breaks the lines of his draperies into angular folds, which fills his skies with twirling clouds, his landscapes with ruined cottages and dashing cascades. It is as part of the rococo that we must regard him; his paintings are fairly judged, not on the bare walls of museums, but on the fantastic panels of their original setting, surrounded by the furniture and the *objets d'art* which are an essential part of the scheme. Boucher was inevitably affected by the romantic ideas of Watteau and his school. In his youth he engraved some of Watteau's paintings, and in his drawings especially strove to catch the incisive light and shade of Watteau's draperies and the full modelling of his virile forms; but these aims were not really in harmony with Boucher's decorative purpose. Sir Joshua Reynolds was amazed, when he visited the Frenchman's studio, to find him painting without reference to the model; for before he had achieved maturity the once brilliant draughtsman had abandoned all attempt to draw inspiration from nature in any form.

The narrowness of his interest in life is revealed by a comparison of his *Musical Contest* in Gallery XVIII with any picture by Watteau, or even by Lancret. Beside the passion of Watteau's rendering, this scene is emptily theatrical, with its exaggerated attitudes, its conventional scenery, its cold, unsympathetic colouring. *The Modiste,* upon the opposite wall, gives us an interesting glimpse into contemporary life. It shows the leisurely morning of a fashionable lady as she idly examines amid the profusion of her bedroom selections from her kneeling modiste's box. But the attempted reality of the scene only emphasises the narrowness of the painter's art—narrow as the idler's own life. Her blue dress and the mauve hangings are hard and monotonous. Scenes of actual life were not of real interest to Boucher, and most of his decorative work derives from the old conventions of the Grand Manner. His treatment of these ideas is entirely of the eighteenth century, but a classical tag at the bottom of almost every picture explains the rudity of the powdered beauties and gives them the respectability of the old tradition. For a few months Boucher was the pupil of Le Moyne, and, though he strenuously denied any obligation to him, he carried on the tradition in which Le Moyne had worked, evolving from it with his own peculiar genius a complete expression of the ideas of his age. He transformed the mock Classical into the true rocaille.

The Grand Manner is to be found in the two huge canvases upon the Grand Staircase, *The Rising* and *The Setting of the Sun*, where Apollo and Thetis gesticulate to one another amid a court of tritons and naiads resting upon the waves. These are Boucher's most ambitious efforts, and so reveal his limitations to the full. The rococo spirit does not suit the grandeur of Olympus; it has long ago sapped the sense of structure and vitality indispensable to figure painting upon such a scale. To the naiads of the foreground, languorously reclining upon the billowing waves, Boucher has imparted the rich plasticity he learnt from Rubens. The fullness of their limbs achieves the voluptuousness he desires, but mere flesh, even of the most dazzling, will not enable Apollo to stand; his strained position painfully reveals the absence of bone or sinew.

These pictures, which belonged to Mme. de Pompadour, were duplicated in tapestries, which have disappeared; Boucher's first employment was as a designer in the Beauvais tapestry manufactory, of which later in life he became inspector. His dual profession was an integral factor in the formation of his art. Tapestry designs were for the most part executed as oil paintings, and thus every oil painting became a potential tapestry design. Such a combination was detrimental to each art, for tapestry became too elaborate and ambitious in its aim, painting correspondingly narrower in its ideals. The identification of the two arts is an illuminating instance of the general tendency of all the arts of the period to borrow too much from one another. In *The Rape of Europa* there is detailed evidence of the influence of tapestry upon painting, for the flowers which are scattered upon the foreground and which wreathe the bull are painted exactly as they are woven upon the Beauvais coverings of many a chair in the Collection.

It is in the series of four decorations in Gallery XIX that we find the painter really at his best, for in these tall rectangular panels he is frankly a decorator and does not aspire to the Grand Manner. In *Cupid a Captive* (illustration), for instance, there is very little attempt at constructing a real scene; the nymph at the top of the group seems to be no farther away than the two in the foreground, and we hardly know upon what her fair body rests. The composition is concocted out of the rococo dictionary rather than observed from life or inspired by any real vision of the artist. A glance round this room shows upon the various pieces of furniture every *motif* which goes to make the picture. The naked nymphs form handles to the vases upon the mantelpiece, Cupids in the form of fire-dogs disport

BOUCHER: CUPID A CAPTIVE.

[p. 120.

themselves below, turtle-doves bill upon the opposite commode; even the water which in the picture flows from the fountain, apparently upon the back of an unconscious nymph, is found in the clock upon the mantelpiece flowing from a pitcher at either side, while the garland of flowers with which Cupid is to be bound is the same which decorates in ormolu a dozen commodes or bestrews in tapestry whole sets of chairs. Boucher is simply one of a host of decorators all using the same conventional *motifs* to produce a harmonious background for a leisured life. He is not an artist in the modern sense of the word, expressing his own emotions or experimenting in his own ideas; he is the servant of an aristocracy providing what is expected of him upon relatively conventional lines. Yet he achieves his purpose with a success unattained by any of his contemporaries in France and evolved out of these conventions a softness and abandon beyond the reach of men with higher ideals. The English are a little too prone to take Rembrandt as their sole criterion, and to expect, like Tolstoy, a moral purpose in every form of art. Yet there is need for many forms of art, and the slighter talent of the decorator is a rare thing not to be despised. In this rôle Boucher was never at a loss; he continued until the very end painting yard upon yard of canvas with a gaiety which only the French know how to create. To criticise him fairly we must judge him by the standard, not of Rembrandt, but of the other great decorators, who make the expression of gaiety their first ambition. But even from this standpoint Boucher is by no means supreme. Tiepolo, who must have influenced his ideas, surpasses him easily in invention and vivacity, and combines an even greater decorative sense with a wittier and more fertile imagination.

The four panels by Boucher in this little room have a story which is a good example of the history enshrined in the Wallace Collection. They were painted for Mme. de Pompadour's boudoir in the Hôtel de l'Arsenal, where she entertained Louis XV, and where his waning attentions had to be revived with the amorous tales which they recite. After Louis XV's death, Louis XVI is said to have been offended by their frank incitements and to have ordered their removal. The gentleman to whom he gave the order obligingly removed them to his own *salon*, and at the Revolution they were despatched for safety abroad. At the Restoration they found their way back to Paris and were finally bought by Lord Hertford set in the form of a screen. They decorated the marquess's bedroom until Sir Richard Wallace brought them to London. There they were set up in Lady Wallace's boudoir, the room where they still hang, and to-day they surround the portrait of the marquise for whom they were painted. This little portrait of Mme. de Pompadour and her spaniel Inés shows how Boucher could paint when he was really interested in his subject. Its very artificiality and elaboration make it an invaluable document of the age. In the face itself there is little idealisation and one feels merely the callous determination which was the royal mistress's strongest characteristic ; but the painting of the dress is superb : a thing so fussy and elaborate would make in most hands a fussy and elaborate picture, but Boucher's dashing strokes, while they render the romance of the elaboration, are so sparingly but so surely placed that the impression remains fresher, more exhilarating than the actual dress can have been. Boucher's finest piece of work was suitably reserved for the lady who made his fortune, and who secured him the position of First Painter after her death.

Oudry

The other great factor in his career was the painter Oudry, an older man who had the favour of Louis XV, and directed the Gobelins and Beauvais manufactories. It was he who gave Boucher his first employment as a tapestry designer. Although he began his career as a portrait painter and was a pupil of Largillière, Oudry was primarily a painter of still life, of animals and of hunting-scenes. It was this gift which won him the favour of the King, who loved hunting even more than women. In Gallery XI (in the centre at the back of the front portion of the building, on the Ground Floor) is a fine series of works of this description. The four *dessus-de-portes* show that his work can be coarse in handling and gloomy in colouring, and the two canvases hung in the window are not of his best. A comparison of one of these, *Dogs and Dead Game*, with the picture over the mantelpiece by Desportes, a painter who belongs equally to the reign of Louis XIV, shows that Oudry was by no means the first of his line. Desportes in turn derives directly from Flemish sources and through his master, one of the many obscure Flemings who crowded Paris in the reign of Louis XIV, forms a link with the great Flemish still-life painters of the seventeenth century. This link is a good instance of the debt the Frenchmen of the eighteenth century owed to Flemish painting. Almost every French Academician studied in Italy, and Raphael and Michelangelo remained to the end the official model of French artists, who derived from them no particle of their craft or inspiration. The complete break between academic theory and actual practice is well summed up in Boucher's famous advice to the young Fragonard, to go to Rome and study Raphael and Michelangelo, but to resist their influence or be lost. Rubens was the main foreign influence upon Watteau and upon Boucher, and in the still-life painters we have another instance of Flemish inspiration. There are many examples in the Wallace Collection of seventeenth-century still-life painting, by Fyt and Snyders the Flemings, and by Weenix and Hondecoeter the Dutchmen, who derive from the same source. In Jan Fyt especially we find richer colouring, a more incisive feeling for the textures of fur or fruit or flowers, more vitality than is to be found in any of the French still-life painters except Chardin, but the decorative value of seventeenth-century still-life is marred by an affectation of the Grand Manner. Heavy masses of light and shade, and inappropriate classic buildings intrude themselves upon the subject. A far more careless artist, Oudry brought to still-life painting a fresh gaiety of colouring far better suited to its treatment. For the dining-room of a French château, where sportsmen are to sit down to breakfast before a day's pleasure in the park, one could hardly imagine decorations more suitable than the two big canvases by Oudry which face one another in this room. In the *Dogs and Dead Game* (illustration) the pink of hollyhocks and hunting nets, the blue-green of sky and leaves stand out with entrancing freshness against the grey of the terrace steps, the cheerful white of the heron's breast and of the dogs. Oudry is at his most vigorous in the drawing of the dog which stands with fore-feet upon the steps ; his brush shows an unerring sympathy with the animal's coat, each stroke following and interpreting the lie of the hair in a vital manner. In the other picture the still-life upon the table, the tray with bottles and glasses especially, is painted, coarsely perhaps, but with a vigour and effect which quickens the blood and would nerve the most timid for the hunting-field.

Boucher owes much of his style to his contact with

Oudry. He had no interest in nature himself, and, just as he adopted his treatment of the human figure from Rubens, so he adopted from Oudry his representation of landscape, his treatment of foliage and flowers, and the light, cheerful colouring which he was the first to apply in figure-painting. The drawings of the two are often confused, and they stand together as the two best representatives of French decoration during Louis XV's reign, the one painter to the King, the other favourite of the royal mistress.

THE LOUIS XVI STYLE

Oudry and Boucher are the typical artists of the Louis XV period; they provided what was asked of them, but in so doing they narrowed to the last degree the ends of art. Their art is built upon the shallowest foundations. Its *motifs* are conventional, its spirit unimaginative and materialistic; and in this it reflects exactly the limitations of the society for which it was created. Art is indeed always the most complete expression of the ideals of a nation or at least of that part of it which is free to express itself. If scholars who pore laboriously over constitutional documents and economic statistics would only visit the Wallace Collection with eyes open to the real meaning of pictures, furniture, and decoration, they would find all the proof they could want, in compact and vivid form, of that which made revolution inevitable. The

OUDRY: DOGS AND DEAD GAME.

[p. 126.

society of the French eighteenth century was an aristocracy such as in England we have never had. To the very eve of the Revolution the French aristocrat held tenaciously to every one of his ancient feudal rights but to none of his feudal duties. The strict despotism of Valois and Bourbon had been built up at the expense of the aristocracy, who had gradually been ousted from any real part in the Government. Valois leadership had been gained by the gradual extinction of rival aristocratic dynasties, and the Bourbons carried on the policy by employing in the direction of the State only men of insignificant extraction, who depended wholly upon their masters and could be depressed as easily as they were raised. Thus the French aristocrat came to have only one field in which he could serve his country, the field of battle. This was amusing enough when Louis XIV was winning his first victories, but it became boring in the eighteenth century when France was losing her continental prestige before the rising power of Prussia, and her colonial possessions before the English forces. Nor could the French aristocrat find an outlet for his energies in private enterprise: his still feudal notions of caste forbade. Seclusion from the realities of life produces occasionally an extraordinary originality of mind, but among the majority it tends to moral stupor and a decline in energy of every kind.

A whole class thus set itself to amusement and the elaboration of luxury as the sole end in life, and the moral lesson of the experiment is to be read in the art which was the result. In the first reaction from the repression of seventeenth century despotism there was vitality enough. Whatever the vices of the rococo and the *fête galante*, they are filled with the exuberance of youth, with the inventive imagination which only the French can bring to the problem of enjoyment. But long before the end of the century, society had spent its youth. There is an illuminating little series of pictures by Lancret in the National Gallery. Four small canvases represent four ages in man's life. In the first three Childhood, Youth, and Maturity are represented by young gallants in fine clothes enjoying the gaieties of love and sport. In the fourth old age is represented by a poor countryman sitting among his family outside his hovel. All the pleasures which the eighteenth century sought were the pleasures of youth. Old age was for the poor, for the rich it did not exist. But youth does not last for ever, and the eighteenth century provided badly for its old age. Before the end of the reign of Louis XV it began to show signs of fatigue. The exuberant curves of furniture changed to flat sides and straight lines, ornament grew mechanical in detail, conventionally symmetrical in design. There was much talk of a classical reaction, but no return to a genuine sense of structure or to finer proportions beneath the elaborate ornament. The Louis XVI style—reigning long before Louis XVI (1774–93)—has matchless delicacy and elaboration, but these are its sole charm. More manly qualities are gone.

Greuze

This utter loss of all virility is nowhere better illustrated than in the work of Greuze. Painters with great ideas create great means, fascinating in themselves, to express them. In Greuze feebleness of execution is paralleled only by confusion of mind. The small picture, *The Inconsolable Widow* (illustration), in Gallery XVIII is a good instance of his shuffling mentality. He has tried his hardest here to gain some intensity both of meaning and of design. The porphyry pedestal which supports the dead husband's bust is represented with faithful care and the colour is pulled together by a timid use of Boucher's pink and blue. The blue of the chair-back is caught up in the ribbon of the lady's hair, the pink of the flowers is pointedly echoed in her cheek and breast, and into the painting of her dress he has striven to put the intensity of Watteau's rendering of satin. But how poor this work appears beside a figure by Watteau. We have seen how Watteau's vivid stabs of light and shade produce more than a scintillating brilliance, they show with unerring accuracy the structure of the form beneath. Greuze's flashy imitation merely confuses it, the light zig-zagging haphazardly in every direction. If one searches for the form beneath, one finds that this poor lady's legs are of impossible length, her whole body out of proportion to her head. The dirty white of the dress is a poor substitute for the pure colours of Watteau's keen imagination and is further dulled by the negative grey of the background. This feeble manner expresses only a confusion of ideas. The title of the picture, and the action of the lady, who leans tearfully towards her dead husband's effigy his last letters in her hand, suggest a moral purpose in the artist's mind ; but this is negatived as much by the insipid pink and blue as by the carefully arranged *décolletage* of the dress. Greuze made the best of both worlds ; he took advantage of the half-hearted reaction of his time towards a sense of moral obligation, but he mingled with it a degree of suggestiveness which makes Boucher's frank sensuality appear almost virtuous. Among the Boucher decorations of the next room, the lady in Greuze's *Broken Mirror* makes an even more absurd appeal. Over a shattered looking-glass the head of a girl of fifteen reveals a childish grief, but it is balanced upon a mature body as ill-proportioned as that of the disconsolate widow. There is the same suggestive disorder in the attire. These two pictures are examples of Greuze's earlier style, when he combined an attempted vigour of execution with a new class of subjects fondly imagined to be of virtuous sentiment. They are boudoir variations of the larger scenes of cottage life, such as *La Lecture de la Bible*, with which he won his first success. That Diderot should have championed his work and proclaimed him the first

GREUZE: THE INCONSOLABLE WIDOW.

[*p.* 130.

French painter to infuse morality into art is only a further proof that the eighteenth century did not know what morality was.

The feebleness of mind which Greuze exhibited in his pictures is an indication of an equal feebleness in the conduct of his life. He married an immature heroine, vapid as one of his own subjects, and lived to learn that this kind of "innocence" means little but an artless appetite for pleasure and a complete incapacity for self-control. The head and shoulder heroines who brought Greuze fame in the nineteenth century carefully reveal bosoms of full maturity and have the heads of young girls of fifteen. Their simulated innocence seems to express no particular virtue so much as an easy yielding to the passions of a dissipated age. Their disproportioned faces measure often as much across the eyes as from chin to forehead and seem to have no head. Even more lifeless than the drawing is the cold and insipid colouring. The earlier version of the *Psyche* in Gallery XX shows a little more energy of expression than is usual in these girls' heads, and a certain breadth of design not unlike that of some of Sir Joshua Reynolds' smaller portraits. Indeed, though the work of the latter has a vigour which puts out of the question any comparison of the two artists, there is a similarity of idea between Greuze's compositions and such pictures as *The Age of Innocence, The Infant Samuel,* or *The Snake in the Grass,* which suggests that there was some connection other than the sentimentality common in the period to the countries of their birth.

Like every other painter Greuze attempted the Grand Manner, but the reception of his first essay in this fashion by the Academy committee, who said they would receive him not for things of that kind but as *peintre de genre*, mortified him so bitterly that he would not exhibit again until after the revolution. In *The Offering to Cupid* in Gallery XX, his most ambitious work at Hertford House, the kneeling figure has not strength to support her dislocated limbs. Colour there is none, and one could hardly find a more painful instance of the degradation to which the Grand Manner had come.

When the painter died in poverty, overtaken by the Revolution, his name was cherished only by Napoleon, who is said to have shed a tear at the news of his death.

Boilly

Another side of eighteenth-century decadence is revealed in the pictures by Boilly in Gallery XX. This painter survived the Revolution and became a favourite of Restoration drawing-rooms. The enthusiasm that had once been felt for fundamental things in art had long disappeared before a delight in the finishing of surfaces. The sculptured clocks, so grandiloquent in pretentious allegory, so elaborate in conception, so rich with gilt and jewels, show a pitiful lack of vitality or design when placed beside the coarsest bronze ornament of the Italian Renaissance. The whole attention of their makers is absorbed in the meticulous chasing of the surface, where each separate texture is rendered by a different use of the chisel. Beneath the surface the eighteenth century did not care to probe. This passion for minute elaboration is characteristic of Boilly's paintings. The porcelain hardness of his silks and satins is achieved with laborious care, but his figures are so shapeless, their attitudes so insipid, that one wonders how they can contrive to stand. Colour, drawing, and design are all equally expressionless.

Fragonard

Yet even at this hour France produced her man of genius. In Fragonard the *ancien régime* "died game," persistently frivolous to the last. His *Pierrot* in Gallery XVIII stands for all that it had striven to enjoy. This little boy in his fancy dress of Watteauesque design, his hands hidden in the long sleeves of his Pierrot costume, his face shaded by the huge sailor hat, expresses none of the deeper qualities of youth, only the freshness of life's spring, its happy, careless enjoyment of the passing hour. The freshness of youth was what the century longed most ardently to preserve, and the whole composition, with its lively pinks and blues exquisitely disposed upon the white dress, holds the secret of perpetual joy. Mr. MacColl once described it perfectly as resembling a bunch of sweet peas. Fragonard, who was Boucher's pupil, has here got the utmost from his master's favourite colour-scheme of pink and blue.

The little landscape at the other end of the same wall, *The Gardens of the Villa d'Este,* belongs to the earliest period of Fragonard's career, when he had visited Rome in deference to the universal custom, doubtless with his tongue in his cheek and Boucher's advice not to take Rome too seriously in his ears. He travelled about Italy and the South of France with the landscape painter Hubert Robert, and together they brought the classical landscape to the last degree of degenerate conventionalism. This little garden scene is a fantasy upon Claude's treatment of trees and his elaboration of tone over a set colour-scheme of blue and green. If Claude is to be blamed for holding aloof from nature, Fragonard certainly got no nearer to her heart; the formal arrangement of trees and terraces resembles the setting of a contemporary ballet. In *The Souvenir,* in which a lady seen in silhouette against the sky carves her message upon the trunk of a tree, the fantasy is in Watteau's manner.

The *Fountain of Love,* upon the opposite wall, must belong to the earlier days of the young painter's return to Paris, when he found critics and painters alike groaning against Boucher's riotous conventionalism and preaching a return to a severer style. In the effort to avoid the beloved pink and blue Fragonard has almost denied colour altogether ; but the heavy greys and browns make the scene a sombre one. The figures which run to drink at the fountain are far from perfectly drawn, but they are cleaner of limb and feature than any that had been seen for some time. Yet in spite of severe intention the true Fragonard dominates the scene, and billowing clouds of the old rococo bear a tumbling swarm of infant Loves.

Each of these pictures is an essay in a different manner, and the essential weakness at the base of Fragonard's art is shown in his inveterate virtuosity. He has no sound anchorage in life. Discovering nothing in it worthy of his deep attention, he is borne along by the stream, exhibiting his grace and brilliance here and there, where fancy touches him, not usually at the call of nature, but at the beckoning of another artist. In *A Young Scholar* one finds him aiming higher. An essay in the manner of Rembrandt results in a smaller measure of success. Utterly opposed to the dainty minuteness and frivolous colouring of the landscape or the *Souvenir* are the large, free strokes, the warm colouring, and the broad handling of light and shade with which this little picture is carried out. Fragonard has been moved by some Rembrandt, but his playful touch will not carry him to Rembrandt's emotional heights. *The Schoolmistress* is a happier rendering in a similar vein. Do not look too deep, do not enquire into this lady's proportions, do not ask why she is keeping school in such a curiously romantic place, or why the piercing beam of light from the grating behind illuminates her so brilliantly from the front, and you will be able to enjoy the whimsical charm of her attitude, of the little boy who stands before her in his vest, and of the horde of peeping children around. "A. B. C. D. E. FRAGONARD" is written upon the slate. This must have been painted after Fragonard had retired with his wife from the frivolities of Paris to found their family in his native Grasse.

But the first picture which made his name in Paris will always be the first by which he is remembered. *The Swing* (illustration)—or, rather, *Les Hazards heureux de l'Escarpolette,* for our English titles have taken half the gaiety from French scenes—represents him at the moment of his most audacious fancy. Nothing can show the utter unreality of this picture better than its origin. It was painted as a portrait of the two central figures. The Baron de St. Julien, a distinguished courtier and dilettante, sent one morning for a respectable Academician called Doyen. He presented the painter to his mistress, and said he wished for a portrait of them both, suggesting the picture in outline much as it is now. His mistress was to be swung through the air by a bishop, while he himself reclined upon the ground beneath in delighted contemplation of the charms exposed. Doyen described himself as petrified at the suggestion and, indeed, a like proof of mockery and dissipation has rarely been planned with such gay deliberation for posterity. Doyen managed in

FRAGONARD: THE SWING

[p. 136.

spite of his shocked feelings to make the additional suggestion of madame's slippers hurtling through the air for Cupid to catch, but he would not undertake the commission himself. He suggested a young fellow called Fragonard, and to Fragonard the task was given. He had the grace to substitute a lacquey for the bishop, and his rendering of the scene was so completely fantastic that the original coarseness of the subject is almost hidden from view. Not a single detail reminds us of nature in any form. The light, which is neither of sun nor of moon, seems with its incredible luxuriance of tone to have coaxed the gnarled and writhing trees to put forth a feverish abundance of foliage, as if for a last round of senile dissipation. The ropes of the swing are not ropes any mortal would trust, suspended as they are from inconsistent points; knotted and decayed, they seem to be a relic from some stranded and forgotten ship. The exuberant detail of the scene is intensified in the lady's figure. The fresh pink of her dress stands out in startling suddenness from the blue-green of the background and emphasises the delightful pattern of her outline; its twirling frills have an incredible animation.

Meretricious as it is in idea and in execution, so extravagant a fancy could never have been produced in a more sober age. Only a hot-house can produce an orchid. Fragonard is the most brilliant of his age, and he conjures up for us the whole romance of its extravagance; but only by making a virtue of its very vices. Its elaborations are the sole attraction of this picture, and it is these very elaborations that come to strangle the deeper things that should have lain beneath. Under this lady's frills her limbs will not fit together ; the sense of structure in which the tradition had begun has collapsed under its overgrown decoration. A narrow convention in colouring has replaced the original wealth of romantic expression. When, after the Revolution, the trappings of the *ancien régime* were cast aside, there was found to be no basis left on which a new generation of artists might build. French painting had to undergo a painful wandering in the wilderness before it reached the new soil of modern art.

THE END

MEDIÆVAL ART. *By* W. R. LETHABY. *With 56 plates.*

THE SCOTTISH SCHOOL OF PAINTING. *By* WILLIAM D. McKAY, R.S.A. *With 46 plates.*

CHRISTOPHER WREN. *By* LENA MILMAN. *With upwards of 60 plates.*

CORREGGIO. *By* T. STURGE MOORE. *With 55 plates.*

ALBERT DURER. *By* T. STURGE MOORE. *With 4 copperplates and 50 half-tone engravings.*

SIR WILLIAM BEECHEY, R.A. *By* W. ROBERTS. *With 49 plates.*

THE SCHOOL OF SEVILLE. *By* W. SENTENACH. *With 50 plates.*

A History of Art

By DR. GIULIO CAROTTI, of the Royal Academy of Fine Arts in Milan and the Royal University of Rome. ENGLISH EDITION revised by MRS. S. ARTHUR STRONG, LL.D. *Each volume fully illustrated. Small crown 8vo., cloth, 6s. net. each.*

VOL. I. ANCIENT ART. 540 *Illustrations.*

VOL. II. THE MIDDLE AGES: Early Christian and Neo-Oriental Art: European Art North of the Alps. 360 *Illustrations.*

VOL. III. ITALIAN ART IN THE MIDDLE AGES. 357 *Illustrations.*

Masters of Painting

Each volume containing 32 photogravure illustrations. Demy 8vo., cloth. 5s. net.

1. RAPHAEL. *By* JULIA CARTWRIGHT (Mrs Ady)
2. BOTTICELLI. *By* JULIA CARTWRIGHT (Mrs. Ady).
3. LEONARDO DA VINCI. *By* DR. GEORG GRONAU.
4. HOLBEIN. *By* FORD MADOX HUEFFER.
5. ROSSETTI. *By* FORD MADOX HUEFFER.

The Popular Library of Art

Each volume containing about 300 pages with 45 illustrations. 16mo. cloth. 2s. 6d. net each.

1. FREDERICK WALKER. *By* CLEMENTINA BLACK.
2. REMBRANDT. *By* AUGUSTE BREAL.
3. VELAZQUEZ. *By* AUGUSTE BREAL.
4. BOTTICELLI. *By* JULIA CARTWRIGHT (Mrs. Ady)
5. RAPHAEL. *By* JULIA CARTWRIGHT (Mrs. Ady).
6. GAINSBOROUGH. *By* ARTHUR B. CHAMBERLAIN.
7. CRUIKSHANK. *By* W. H. CHESSON.
8. BLAKE. *By* G. K. CHESTERTON.
9. G. F WATTS. *By* G. K. CHESTERTON.
10. ALBRECHT DURER. *By* LINA ECKENSTEIN.
11. THE ENGLISH WATER-COLOUR PAINTERS. *By* A. J. FINBERG.
12. HOGARTH. *By* EDWARD GARNETT.
13. LEONARDO DA VINCI. *By* DR. GEORG GRONAU.
14. HOLBEIN. *By* FORD MADOX HUEFFER.
15. ROSSETTI. *By* FORD MADOX HUEFFER.
16. THE PRE-RAPHAELITE BROTHERHOOD. *By* FORD MADOX HUEFFER.
17. PERUGINO. *By* EDWARD HUTTON.
18. THE FRENCH IMPRESSIONISTS. *By* CAMILLE MAUCLAIR.
19. WATTEAU. *By* CAMILLE MAUCLAIR.
20. MILLET. *By* ROMAIN ROLLAND.
21. WHISTLER. *By* BERNHARD SICKERT.

Gallery VIII
Renaissance Cabinets

Carlton Louis XV furniture on first floor

Gallery ~~IX~~ Mr R. Romney.

Gallery XVI Strawberry Girl Reynolds
— — Dance Poussin
— — Landscape Lorrain
— — Rubens

Gallery ~~I~~ Protector Somerset
— — Louis XIV Largillière
Gallery IX Mary Q of Scots

Mlle de C. Nattier
Comtesse de Tillières Nattier
Fête in a Park Watteau

Gallery ~~XVIII~~
~~Champs~~ Elysées Watteau
Music Party "
Harlequin & Columbine "
Mlle Camargo Lancret
Gallery XX La Belle Grecque "

Italian Comedians by a Fountain Lancret
Offering to Cupid Greuze
Gallery XXI
Bonn.